Canon EOS R10 User Companion

Your Indispensable Handbook with Illustrations to Master the EOS R10

By

Mats Sauer

Table of Content

INTRODUCTION

Canon introduced new cameras and lenses loved by Canon users and even people with other camera brands. Now, they've made smaller cameras, like the EOS R10, which this book is about. The R-system is a new type of camera that's just as good as regular digital SLRs. It comes in different models like EOS R3, R5, R6 II, R10, and R7. Canon has many lenses and accessories for these cameras, and they're planning to release even more in the future.

Canon has made a lot of different lenses and camera accessories that work with their new camera. They did it fast and now have a big and complete system. Canon's R-series cameras aren't the first mirrorless ones they made; that title goes to their EOS M cameras, which were small but could have been more flexible. The R-series, including your camera, was designed based on what Canon learned, catering to serious photographers and professionals.

You might wonder, how do I use this camera? Canon's manual is complicated, and online tutorials only cover some things well. Who wants to learn from a screen? Do you want to watch videos or go out and take pictures?

Canon's big instruction books in PDF form are packed with info, but they need to explain why you should use specific settings or features. They're hard to navigate, and you have to flip between different sections a lot. Plus, the basic manual has not-so-great black-and-white drawings and small pictures that need to show the camera's capabilities better.

I made this Canon EOS R10 Guide unique. It uses big, colorful pictures to show you buttons and their functions. I explain things in detail, avoiding generic advice like other guides. There are no long chapters on shooting landscapes or portraits, so you get specific and helpful information.

This book helps you learn how to use your camera to take different kinds of pictures. Instead of just telling you where to stand to capture a specific moment, it teaches you how to adjust settings like autofocus, shutter speed, and flash to capture great sports photos in any situation.

Some readers want less basic photography info on my blog. But others who are learning photography want my help to understand their cameras better.

I wrote this book to help both beginners and experienced photographers. If you're new, you'll learn how to use the camera's features. If you're experienced, you might discover some helpful photography tips. I want to assist everyone, whether you're just starting or have taken photos for a long time.

CHAPTER 1: GETTING THE CAMERA UP AND RUNNING

Preparing the Camera for Initial Use

Setting up your camera is quick and straightforward. First, charge the battery, attach the lens, adjust the viewfinder, insert and format a memory card, and make a few settings. If you've used a similar Canon camera before, it's easy because you already know the steps. I'll explain in more detail for beginners.

Power Options

To use your Canon EOS R10 camera, ensure its battery is charged. The camera comes with an LP-E17 battery pack. A fully charged battery can take about 210 to 450 photos, depending on whether you use the screen or viewfinder to take pictures. This estimate follows standard tests by the Camera & Imaging Products Association.

Rechargeable camera batteries lose power even when not in use. It happens because of a chemical reaction inside the battery. If you bought your camera, the battery might not be fully charged. It would help if you charged it before you start taking lots of pictures.

There are different chargers for your camera, but most people prefer the small LC-E17 charger. If you buy an extra charger, you not only get more features but also have a backup in case your main charger stops working. An extra charger is helpful when you need to charge multiple batteries together.

Here are your power options:

- **LC-E17:** This charger is for cameras, including older models with LC-E17 batteries. It's handy because it's small, plugs directly into your power socket, and doesn't need a cord. A blinking light shows it's charging the battery.

- **LC-E17E:** This charger, like the LC-E17, charges one battery, but it needs a cord. It can be useful if your power outlet is hard to reach. You can plug in the cord and place the charger on your desk. The cord is standard and works with various devices. I bought multiple cords and plugged them into different places in my home. I can use these cords to charge my camera, laptop, and other devices without reaching behind furniture. The cord doesn't use electricity when nothing is connected to it. Remember to unplug your charger when you're not charging your devices.

The USB Power Adapter PD-E1 costs around $140 and lets you charge LPE6NH camera batteries using a USB-C cable without taking them out of the camera. I've used a cheaper third-party USB-C charger successfully. It follows a specific charging standard and can provide different power levels. Regular USB chargers don't work and might show an error, but you can fix it by turning off the camera and removing the battery for a few minutes.

When you charge the camera with USB, it has to be turned off. While charging, a green light in the lower-right corner of the camera will be on. This light is the same one that blinks red when the camera is saving photos. Once charging is done, the light goes off.

The DC coupler DR-E18 and AC adapter AC-E6N are tools that let you use your camera without a battery by plugging it directly into an electrical outlet. The coupler, costing around $50, fits into the battery space of your camera and has a cord coming out of it. This cord connects to the AC adapter, priced at $100, which provides the power your camera needs.

Photographers in studios take many pictures for a long time and need a constant power source. They use cords and adapters to keep their cameras and lights powered up. This setup is essential for studio photography, video shooting, and other special photo techniques.

Charging the Battery

When you put the battery in the charger correctly, a light starts blinking. It blinks until the battery is half charged, then blinks differently until it's 75% charged, and then in another way until it's 90% charged, usually taking about 90 minutes. To be sure it's fully charged, leave it for another hour until the light turns green. Once charged, put the battery in your camera. To remove it, press a button.

Mounting a Lens

To keep your camera safe and dust-free, first, choose the lens you want to use. Loosen the back cap of the lens without removing it. Store the lens vertically in your camera bag's slot for quick access, ensuring it's protected. Remove the cap before attaching the lens to keep the lens clean until the last moment.

First, turn the cap near the button to take it off. Always use the cap when there's no lens to keep dust out of the camera. Dust can harm the camera's insides, especially the sensor. The cap also protects the sensor from damage by objects, even your fingers, if you're not careful.

1. Take off the caps from the camera and lens.

2. Put the lens on the camera, matching the red marks.

3. Turn the lens to secure it.

4. Set lens settings to autofocus and stabilizer on.

5. If the lens hood is reversed, twist it to the right position.

6. The hood protects the lens and reduces glare from light outside the picture area.

Adjusting Diopter Correction

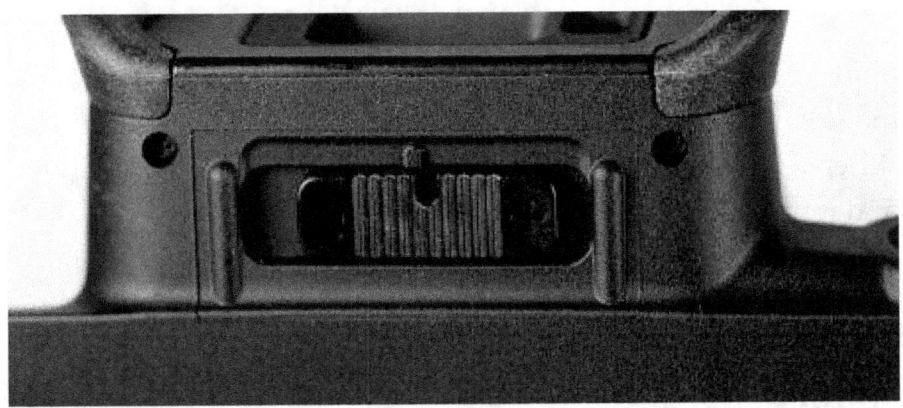

If your eyesight isn't perfect, you can use your camera's diopter adjustment to see clearly without glasses. If you wear glasses, you can adjust the slider near the viewfinder until everything looks sharp, allowing you to work without your glasses.

Inserting a Memory Card

To take pictures, you need to put a memory card in your camera. Open the compartment door at the bottom, but make sure the camera is turned off. Put the memory card in the slot with the label facing the back of the camera. The part with the metal contacts goes in first.

The slot works with super-fast SD cards, transferring data at speeds up to 300Mbs. You can also use slower SD cards, but different brands have different speed specs. Write speed is how fast the device saves photos, while read speed is how quickly photos are transferred to your computer using a fast connection like USB 3.x.

Shut the door, and your preflight checklist is finished! (Just make sure to take off the lens cap when you're taking a picture!) When you need to take out the memory card later, push it down, and it will pop out.

Exploring External Camera Features

Topside controls

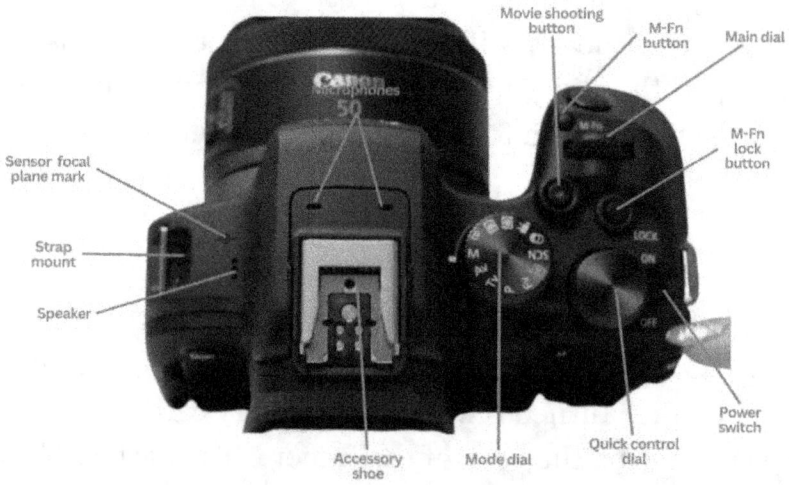

- **MENU button:** Displays the camera's menu on the LCD screen or electronic viewfinder. Press again to exit the menu.

- **Dioptric adjustment:** The dioptric adjustment allows you to correct for your vision when using the viewfinder.

To adjust the dioptric adjustment, slide the lever on the underside of the viewfinder until you can see the viewfinder display clearly.

- **Viewfinder eyepiece:** Peer through the eyepiece to frame your shots. The eyecup/frame blocks out extraneous light and protects your glasses from scratches. The R10's electronic viewfinder has 2,360,000 pixels.

- **Viewfinder sensor:** Detects when your eye approaches the viewfinder and automatically switches the camera from the LCD screen to the viewfinder. You can configure the camera to switch only manually in the Set-up 4 menu.

- **Zoom scale:** Shows the current zoom focal length. (Only available on zoom lenses!)

- **M-Fn button:** This multi-function button has two uses:

  o **Dial functions:** Press the button to display a list of functions. Turn the Main Dial to select a function, then turn the Quick Control Dial to adjust its setting.

  o **Autofocus area selection mode:** Press the AF point selection button on the back of the camera to activate this mode. Assign functions to the M-Fn button using the Custom Controls feature.

- **M-Fn lock button:** Locks certain controls to prevent them from being changed accidentally. Press again to unlock them. You can choose to lock the Main Dial, QCD, Multi-controller, touch control panel, or control ring.

- **Main Dial:** The Main Dial is used to make many shooting settings, such as shutter speed and aperture. It is also used to navigate menus and select images in playback.

  When settings come in pairs, such as shutter speed and aperture in Manual shooting mode, the Main Dial is used for one setting and the Quick Control Dial is used for the other setting.

- **Movie shooting button:** The movie shooting button starts and stops video recording. You can reassign this button to perform another function if you like. To reassign the movie shooting button, go to the Custom Controls feature.

- **Speaker:** Emits audio from the camera, such as video playback and menu tones.

- **Microphones:** Capture sound during video recording.

- **Accessory shoe:** The accessory shoe allows you to attach an electronic flash or other accessory to the camera. To attach an accessory to the accessory shoe, slide it into the shoe and lock it in place.

- **Sensor focal plane mark:** The sensor focal plane mark is a small symbol on the side of the pentaprism that marks the exact location of the sensor's focal plane. This information is useful for precision macro and scientific photography.

- **Strap mount:** The strap mount on either side of the camera allows you to attach a neck strap. To attach a neck strap, thread one end of the strap through the strap mount and then thread the other end of the strap through the loop on the other side of the camera.

- **Power switch:** The power switch turns the camera on or off. To turn the camera on, slide the power switch to the ON position. To turn the camera off, slide the power switch to the OFF position.

- **Mode Dial:** The Mode Dial allows you to select an exposure mode or one of the camera's user settings. To select an exposure mode, turn the Mode Dial to the desired exposure mode. To select a user setting, turn the Mode Dial to the C1, C2, or C3 position, then use the Main Dial to select the desired user setting..

Front features

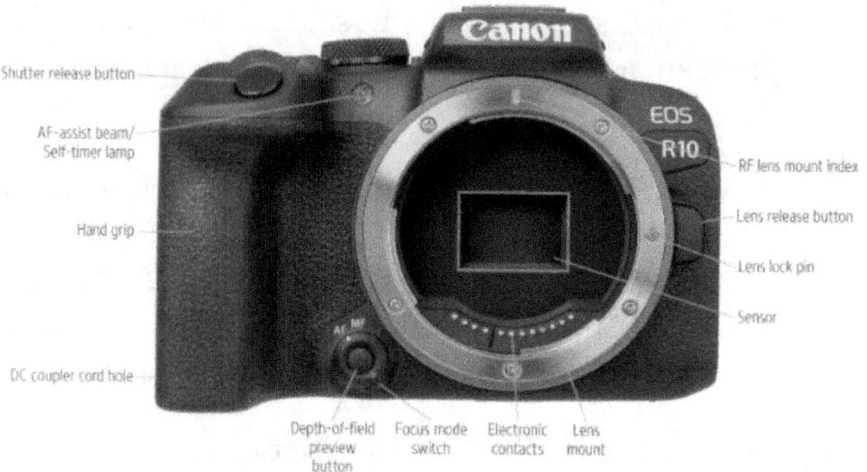

- **Shutter release button:** The shutter release button is located on the top plate of the camera, angled to the right. It is a large, round button, with a soft texture for easy grip. To take a photo, press the shutter release button all the way down. To focus and lock the exposure before taking a photo, press the shutter release button halfway down.

  If the camera is turned off, pressing the shutter release button halfway will turn it on and activate autofocus and autoexposure. If a review image is displayed on the LCD screen, pressing the shutter release button will remove the image from the display and reactivate autofocus and autoexposure.

- **AF-assist beam/Self-timer lamp:** This LED is located on the front of the camera, below the lens mount. It flashes when needed to provide additional illumination for autofocus, or to indicate that the remote control has connected, or when using the self-timer to mark the countdown until the photo is taken.

- **DC coupler cord hole:** This hole is located on the right side of the hand grip, next to the battery compartment door. It is covered by a rubber flap when not in use. To connect the DC coupler DR-E18 to the camera, open the rubber flap and insert the power cable into the hole. Then, close the rubber flap and secure it with the latch.

- **Hand grip:** The hand grip is a large, textured area on the right side of the camera. It provides a comfortable and secure grip for holding the camera. The battery compartment is located inside the hand grip. To access the battery compartment, open the battery compartment door on the bottom of the hand grip.

- **Depth-of-field preview button:** The depth-of-field preview button is located on the front of the camera, below the lens mount. It is a small, black button with a magnifying glass icon on it. To preview the depth-of-field, press the depth-of-field preview button while looking through the viewfinder. The lens will stop down to the aperture that will be used to take the photo, allowing you to see how much of the scene will be in focus.

- **Focus mode switch:** The focus mode switch is located on the top plate of the camera, next to the shutter release button. It has two positions: MF (manual focus) and AF (autofocus). To switch between manual and autofocus, rotate the focus mode switch to the desired position.

- **Lens mount:** The lens mount is located on the front of the camera, below the viewfinder. It is a sturdy flange with a bayonet mount that allows you to attach and remove lenses. To attach a lens, align the lens mount index mark on the lens with the red detent on the camera body. Then, rotate the lens clockwise until it clicks into place. To remove a lens, press the lens release button and rotate the lens counterclockwise until it stops.

- **Lens release button:** The lens release button is located on the lens mount, next to the lens mount index mark. It is a small, black button with a lock icon on it. To remove a lens, press and hold the lens release button while rotating the lens counterclockwise.

- **Lens lock pin:** The lens lock pin is located on the lens flange, next to the lens release button. It is a small pin that retracts when the lens release button is pressed. The lens lock pin prevents the lens from accidentally detaching from the camera body.

- **RF lens mount index:** The RF lens mount index is a small white mark located on the lens mount, next to the lens release button. It is used to align the lens with the camera body when mounting it. To mount a lens, align the RF lens mount index on the lens with the red detent on the camera body. Then, rotate the lens clockwise until it clicks into place.

- **Sensor:** The sensor is located inside the camera body, behind the lens mount. It is a light-sensitive chip that captures the image. Be careful not to touch the sensor when the lens is removed.

- **Electronic contacts:** The electronic contacts are located on the lens mount, next to the RF lens mount index. They connect to matching points on the lens to allow the camera and lens to communicate electronically.

- **Lens hood bayonet:** The lens hood bayonet is a grooved mount that rings the front of the lens. It is used to attach and remove lens hoods. Lens hoods are designed to block extraneous light from entering the lens, which can reduce contrast and cause flare. It is a good idea to always use a lens hood when shooting.

- **Lens hood alignment mark:** The lens hood alignment mark is a small white mark located on the lens hood bayonet. It is used to align the lens hood with the lens when attaching it.

- **Control ring:** The control ring is a programmable ring located on the lens. It can be used to change aperture, shutter speed, ISO, and exposure compensation.

- **Focus ring:** The focus ring is a ring located on the lens. It is used to focus manually or fine-tune autofocus.

- **Zoom ring:** The zoom ring is a ring located on the lens. It is used to zoom in and out.

- **Image stabilizer switch:** The image stabilizer switch is a switch located on the lens. It is used to turn image stabilization on and off. Image stabilization helps to reduce camera shake, which can blur your photos. It is a good idea to use image stabilization whenever possible.

- **Autofocus/Manual focus switch:** The autofocus/manual focus switch is a switch located on the lens. It is used to switch between autofocus and manual focus.

- **Terminal covers:** The terminal covers are rubber covers that protect the camera's interface terminals from dust and moisture.

- **USB Type-C digital terminal:** The USB Type-C digital terminal is used to connect the camera to a computer or other device. It can also be used to charge the camera's battery.

- **HDMI micro OUT terminal:** The HDMI micro OUT terminal is used to connect the camera to an HDMI-compatible television, video recorder, or other device.

- **Headphone terminal:** The headphone terminal is used to connect headphones or other audio playback gear.

- **External microphone IN terminal:** The external microphone IN terminal is used to connect an external microphone.

- **Remote control terminal:** The remote control terminal is used to connect a wired remote control.

Back-of-the-body controls

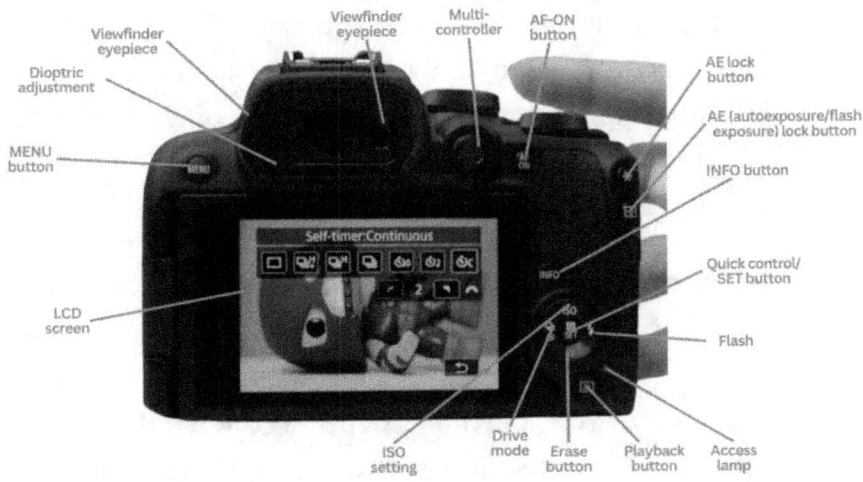

- **Quick Control Dial:** The Quick Control Dial is a rotating dial located on the top plate of the camera, between the shutter release button and the mode dial. It is used to select shooting options, such as f/stop, shutter speed, ISO, and exposure compensation. It can also be used to navigate through menus and to adjust other settings.

  To select a shooting option, rotate the Quick Control Dial until the desired option is highlighted in the viewfinder or on the LCD screen. Then, press the Quick Control Dial to confirm the selection.

- **AF-ON button:** The AF-ON button is located on the back of the camera, below the Quick Control Dial. It is used to activate the autofocus system without having to partially depress the shutter release button. This is useful for situations where you want to separate focus and exposure, such as when you are using back-button autofocus or when you are shooting in manual mode. To activate autofocus, press the AF-ON button. To release autofocus, press the AF-ON button again.

- **AE lock button:** The AE lock button is located on the back of the camera, next to the AF-ON button. It is used to lock the exposure, or flash exposure, that the camera sets when you partially depress the shutter release button. This is useful for situations where you want to lock the exposure before recomposing your shot, or when you are shooting in manual mode.

To lock the exposure, press the AE lock button. The exposure lock indication (*) will appear in the viewfinder and on the LCD screen. To release the exposure lock, press the AE lock button again. When using external flash, pressing the AE lock button will fire a pre-flash, which allows the flash to calculate and lock the exposure before taking the picture.

- **AF point selection/AF point movement/Magnify/Reduce button**

This button has three functions:

  - **AF area mode selection:** Press the button once, then press the M-Fn button repeatedly to switch between the available AF area modes, including Spot AF, 1-Point AF, Expand AF Area AF, Expand AF Area (Around), Flexible Zone AF 1, Flexible Zone AF 2 (vertical), Flexible Zone AF 3 (horizontal), and Whole Area AF.

  - **AF point movement:** Press and hold the button, then use the directional controls to move the AF point or zone around the frame in all AF area modes except Whole Area AF.

  - **Magnify/Reduce:** Press the button once to magnify the view by 5X, press the button again to magnify the view by 10X, and press the button a third time to return to 1X (full-frame) view. While the image is magnified, you can move the zoomed area using the directional controls.

- **Shooting mode:** To magnify the view in shooting mode, press the Magnify/Reduce button once. Then, press the INFO button to magnify the view by 5X. Press the INFO button again to magnify the view by 10X. To return to the full-frame view, press the INFO button a third time. While the image is magnified, you can move the zoomed area using the Multi-controller. To do this, press the Multi-controller in the direction you want to move the zoomed area.

- **Playback mode:** To magnify an image in playback mode, press the Magnify/Reduce button and release it. Then, rotate the Main Dial clockwise to zoom in on the image. You can zoom in to a magnification of up to 15X.

  To zoom out, rotate the Main Dial counterclockwise. To return to the full-frame view, continue to rotate the Main Dial counterclockwise until you reach the Index view. In the Index view, you can see a grid of 4, 9, 36, or 100 images. To view a full-frame view of the currently highlighted image, press the SET button.

- **Multi-controller:** The Multi-controller is a joystick-like button located on the back of the camera. It can be shifted in eight different directions to adjust focus points, move a zoomed area, navigate menus, and other functions. To press the Multi-controller, press down on the center of the joystick.

- **Q/SET button:** The Q/SET button is a multi-function button located on the back of the camera, to the right of the Multi-controller. It has two main functions:

  ○ **In shooting mode:** Press the Q/SET button to display the Quick Control screen. This screen gives you access to a variety of shooting settings, such as white balance, drive mode, and ISO speed.

  ○ **In playback mode:** Press the Q/SET button to display the Playback Quick Control screen. This screen gives you access to a variety of playback options, such as image protection, rating, and cropping.

  To confirm a setting on the Quick Control screen, press the Q/SET button again.

- **Drive mode:** The drive mode determines how many photos the camera will take in a row when you press the shutter release button. To access the drive mode settings, press the left edge of the pad surrounding the Q/SET button.

The following drive modes are available:

○ **Single shooting:** The camera will take one photo each time you press the shutter release button.

○ **Continuous shooting:** The camera will continue to take photos while you hold down the shutter release button.

○ **Self-timer:** The camera will take a photo after a set delay.

• **ISO setting:** The ISO setting determines how sensitive the camera is to light. To access the ISO setting, press the top edge of the pad surrounding the Q/SET button. Higher ISO settings make the camera more sensitive to light, but they can also introduce noise into your images. Lower ISO settings make the camera less sensitive to light, but they also produce cleaner images.

• **Flash:** The flash setting determines when the camera's built-in flash will fire. To access the flash setting, press the right edge of the pad surrounding the Q/SET button.

The following flash settings are available:

○ **Auto:** The camera will automatically fire the flash when needed.

○ **On:** The flash will always fire.

○ **Off:** The flash will never fire.

- **Access lamp:** The access lamp is a small red light located on the back of the camera, below the Q/SET button. This light indicates when the camera is accessing the memory card.

- **Erase/Trash button:** The Erase/Trash button is located on the back of the camera, to the left of the Playback button. This button is used to delete images in playback mode. To delete an image, press the Erase/Trash button. You will then be prompted to confirm the deletion.

- **Playback button:** The Playback button is located on the back of the camera, to the right of the Erase/Trash button. This button is used to display the most recent image in playback mode.

- **INFO button:** The INFO button is located on the back of the camera, to the left of the Q/SET button. This button is used to change the type of information displayed in shooting and playback modes.

In shooting mode, the INFO button can be used to display the following information:

  - Exposure settings

  - Shooting mode

  - Drive mode

  - ISO setting

27

- o Flash setting

- o White balance setting

- o Metering mode

In playback mode, the INFO button can be used to display the following information:

- o File name

- o File size

- o Creation date and time

- o Shooting mode

- o Exposure settings

- o ISO setting

- o Flash setting

- o White balance setting

- o Metering mode

Changing Settings via the Quick Control Screen

The Quick Control screen is a fast way to change up to 17 different camera settings. To access the settings, use the directional controls to move the highlight from one icon to the next. The highlight will wrap around to the next column when it reaches the edge of the screen. Once you've highlighted the setting you want to change, use the left/right directional buttons or either dial to choose from the options at the bottom of the screen. You can also tap the icons on the touch screen to change settings.

There is a second Quick Control screen available when reviewing images in Playback mode. In Shooting mode, the available options vary depending on whether you're using the Quick Control screen or the graphic version. The options in the standard Quick Control screen include:

- **AF area:** Pick the part of the frame where the camera will automatically focus.

- **AF operation:** Pick either One-Shot or Servo mode.

- **Image quality:** Pick between RAW and JPEG file types and choose from Large, Medium, or Small sizes.

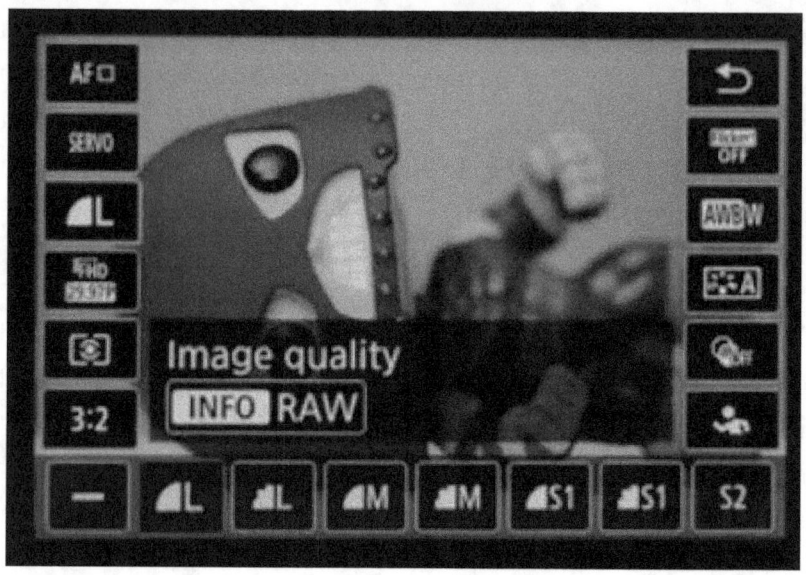

- **Movie recording size:** Choose between very clear 4K videos at 24 or 30 frames per second or sharp Full HD videos at 24, 30, or 60 frames per second.

- **Metering mode:** Choose the part where the camera gathers light details.

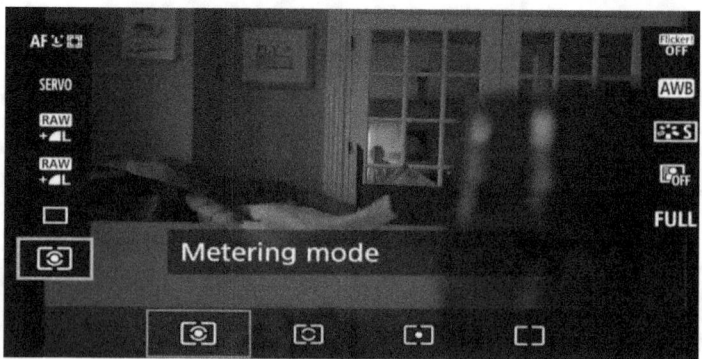

- **Aspect ratio:** You can choose different shapes for photos, like rectangles or squares. Some common shapes are 3:2, 4:3, and 16:9. The last three shapes are cut from the 3:2 shape.

- **Anti-flicker:** Reduce the flickering from certain lights.

- **White balance:** Choose different settings for the color tone, like Daylight or Indoor lighting.

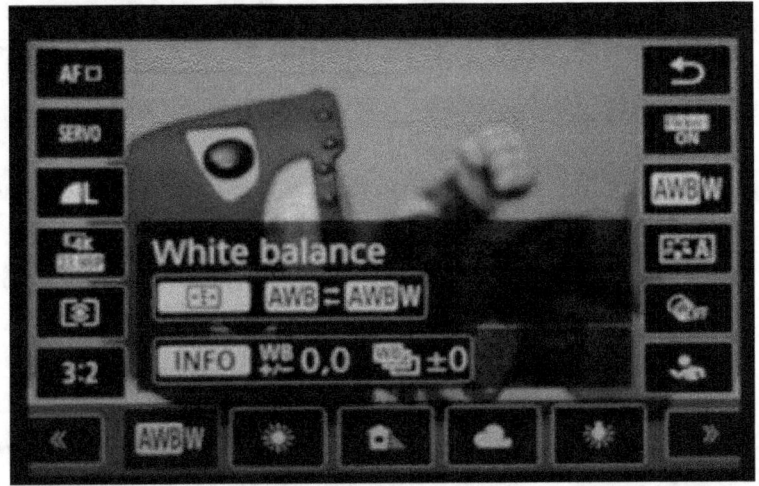

- **Picture style:** In easy words, it means adjusting and improving your photos using specific settings while taking pictures.

- **Creative filters:** Pick one of the special effects I talked about before.

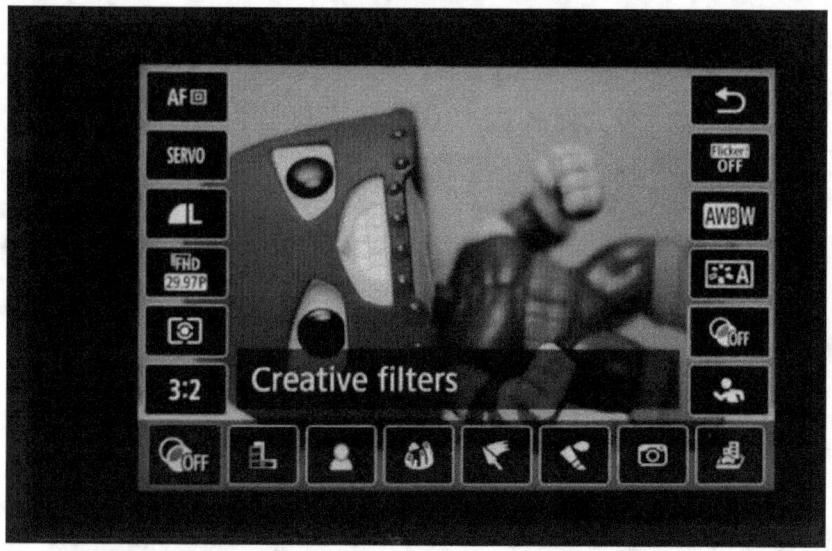

- **Subject to detection:** Choose whether the camera should focus on people, animals, vehicles, or nothing. The graphics screen Quick Control has more choices, and some, like Subject Detection, are removed.

- **Shutter speed:** You can set how fast the camera takes a picture on the Quick Control screen. You can choose between 30 seconds and 1/4000th of a second or let the camera decide automatically. If you're using Manual mode, you can pick both settings, but in Shutter-priority mode, you can only choose the shutter speed.

- **Aperture:** Choose any aperture setting, from the lens's biggest to smallest, when using Manual or Aperture-priority modes.

- **ISO:** In simple words, in photography, you can let the camera automatically adjust the sensitivity to light (Auto ISO), or you can set specific light sensitivity levels up to ISO 25600.

- **Exposure compensation/Auto exposure bracketing:** In simpler words, you can change the brightness of your camera or take multiple shots at different brightness levels in specific camera settings. Adjusting how bright or dim a photo looks when using a flash. You can change flash settings here.

- **Picture Style:** Make your pictures look better by creating and using your photo styles.

- **White balance:** Pick either a ready-made or your white balance setting.

- **White balance shift/bracketing:** Adjust the colors in your photo until they look right.

- **Auto Lighting Optimizer:** Here, you can set up automatic adjustments for brightness and contrast.

- **Wi-Fi/Bluetooth connection:** Allows you to use wireless features easily.

- **Custom controls:** You can change how buttons and dials work by going to different screens.

Formatting Memory Cards

You can try out the new buttons I showed you by setting up a memory card. There are three ways to make an empty card for your camera, but two of them need to be corrected. Here are the right and wrong options:

- **Transfer (move) files to your computer:** When you move pictures from your camera's memory card to your computer, the card gets empty. But if you mark some pictures as protected or if there are damaged parts on the card, those won't be erased. It's best to erase everything on the card before using it again, except if you want to keep some pictures for a bit longer to show others.

- **(Don't) Format on your computer:** To make it simple: If you want to clear your camera's memory card, don't use your computer. Your camera might not like the way the computer does it. The best way is to let the camera itself format the card. Only use your computer if the card is messed up and the camera can't fix it.

- **Set up menu format:** To format a memory card correctly, follow these steps:

  1. Push the MENU button.

  2. Press the INFO button until you see a yellow wrench icon on one of the menus.

3. Turn the big dial to pick the Setup 1 menu.

4. Turn the knob on top of the camera to move down the menu until you reach 'Format Card' under Setup 1.

5. Push the SET button to make your choice official.

6. Turn the QCD to show OK, then press SET to begin formatting. If needed, press INFO before for a thorough cleanup if the card is heavily used.

CHAPTER 2: CONTROLLING FOCUS AND DEPTH OF FIELD

Choosing a Focus Mode

You can change the focus on your camera by moving the switch on the lens or using the camera's switch. But in specific modes, you must still pick how the camera focuses.

To make your camera focus automatically, go to the screen where you see the camera view or the Quick Control menu. Look for the icon that lets you choose how the camera focuses; it might be called One-Shot or Servo.

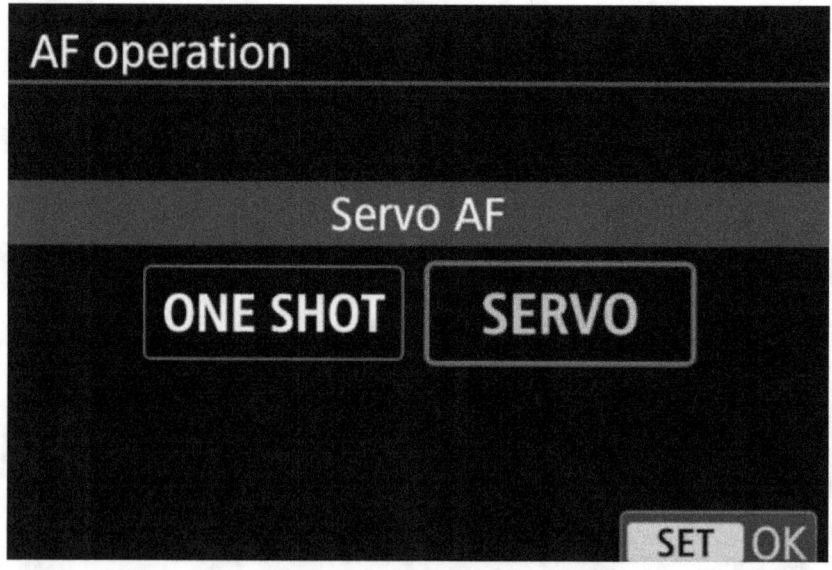

If you set your lens to manual focus, these options won't be there, and you'll see an MF indicator instead.

- **One-Shot:** This mode focuses your camera on a specific point when you press the shutter button halfway. If it's focused, you'll see green boxes, but if not, you'll see orange boxes. The focus stays until you release the button or take the photo. It's great for still subjects.

- **Servo:** Simply put, this mode in a camera focuses when you press the button halfway and keeps adjusting focus if the camera or the subject moves. It's great for capturing sports or anything in motion.

AF Operation

This mode in a camera focuses when you press the button halfway and keeps adjusting focus if the camera or the subject moves. It's great for capturing sports or anything in motion.

The camera can focus in different ways: manually (you adjust it yourself) or automatically using two modes: One-Shot AF (for still subjects) and Servo AF (for moving subjects). You can also zoom in up to 10 times to focus manually precisely. I'll explain these in detail later. Picking the right focus mode and points is crucial for good photos. Using the wrong mode might focus on the wrong thing in your pictures.

Back in the old days, when I used a camera with autofocus for sports photography, I took pictures of baseball players. Some photos turned out well because the background didn't confuse the camera. But when I took pictures of a young pitcher, the camera focused on the fans instead. I only realized this mistake once the film was developed. If I had adjusted the focus manually, the pictures would have been better.

To save battery, the camera won't focus until you press the button halfway. After pressing the button, you can control the focus using different settings. First, decide between One-Shot or Servo. In non-auto modes, press Q/SET, go to AF Operation, and choose One-Shot or Servo using the dials. Ensure the AF/M switch on the camera or lens is set to AF before changing the autofocus mode.

One-Shot AF

In this mode, the camera focuses once until you take the picture or release the button. It's best for still subjects, but you might miss spontaneous moments because the camera takes a moment to focus. This mode uses less battery power.

When the camera is in sharp focus, a green light flashes, and it beeps (unless you turn off the beep sound). If you're using a specific metering mode, the exposure is fixed, too. You can adjust the picture framing without losing focus or exposure by keeping the shutter button halfway pressed. If the camera can't focus, an orange light shows, and you can't take a picture even if you press the button.

One-Shot AF makes focusing easy and quick. You can keep the focus in the center, point at your subject, lock the focus, and move the subject without worrying about adjusting the focus point manually. It saves time and effort.

If you need to take a quick picture without waiting for the camera to focus, you can change the setting. Usually, the camera focuses before taking a shot, but you can make it take the picture right away, even if it's not perfectly focused.

Servo AF

Continuous autofocus is the mode you use for fast-moving things like sports. When you press the shutter button halfway, the camera focuses on the chosen point and adjusts if the subject moves. It's great for capturing action without any beeping noises.

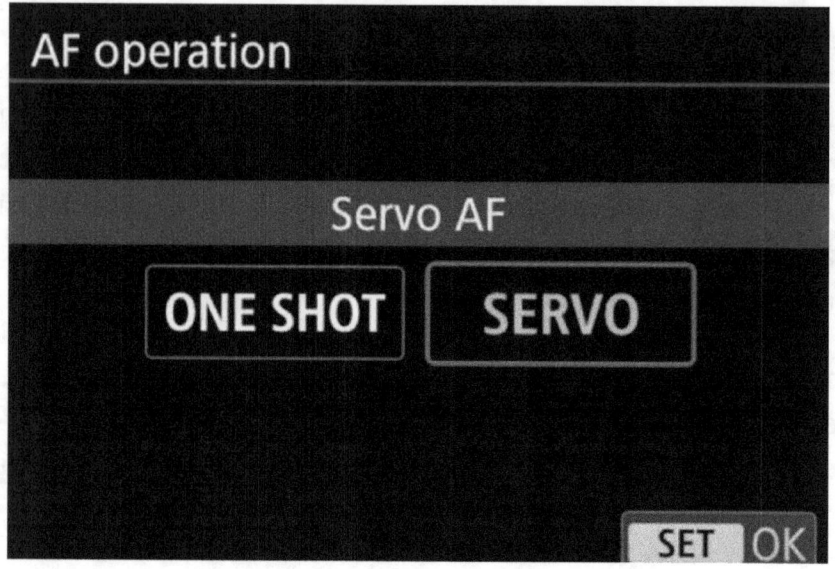

When you press the camera button halfway, it locks focus and exposure. In Servo AF mode, there's almost no delay when you press the button to take a photo. But it uses more battery since it keeps focusing when the button is half-pressed. If you're in Auto mode and the camera detects movement, it switches to this quick focusing mode.

You'll often see continuous autofocus referred to as release-priority because that's the way it has been traditionally used. In that mode, if you press the shutter release down while the system is refining focus, the camera will take a picture, even if the image is slightly out of focus. Servo AF is a smart camera feature that predicts where to focus when a moving object is coming closer or moving away. It figures out the right focus point, either by itself or where you tell it to focus.

Release-priority mode means the camera can take a picture even if it's not perfectly focused. The photo might still turn out clear or slightly blurry.

Manual Focus

You can manually focus your camera by switching it to MF mode, but it takes longer and can be tricky. It saves battery, but focusing on each photo is slower. Canon offers some assistance with manual focus.

Ways to focus better on your include:

- **Focus peaking:** You can make your image outlines stand out by using MF Peaking in the AF 5 menu. You can choose a contrasting color and decide how strong you want the effect (High, Medium, or Low). But remember, peaking won't show up when you zoom in.

- **Magnified view:** The zoomed-in view makes it easier to focus manually, and you can do this even when using autofocus modes, as explained later in this chapter.

Subject Tracking

Your camera, the EOS R10, automatically focuses on things using specific rules. It focuses on close objects and predicts where to focus next based on moving things. When you use different modes, the focus area is green or blue. If you want to know where it's focusing, press the shutter button halfway. It is handy when you're using specific focus options that cover a lot of the picture.

If you use a specific focus method on your camera, you can make it follow a subject automatically. It means when you press the halfway button on the camera, it will keep focusing on and tracking that subject even if it moves. There are different settings you can adjust for this feature in the camera menu.

You can choose from these:

- **Subject Tracking**

  You can pick either "On" or "Off.". If you press the INFO button while selecting a specific area, You can choose to keep track of subjects or not; it's up to you. But be aware if you change the setting in the menu, it applies to all areas.

  When you're tracking something, like a moving object, remember that tracking and the specific area you're focusing on are not the same. For instance, if you choose a focus area on the left side of the frame and your subject moves elsewhere, the tracking will still follow it, even if it's outside the chosen focus area.

- **Subject to Detect**

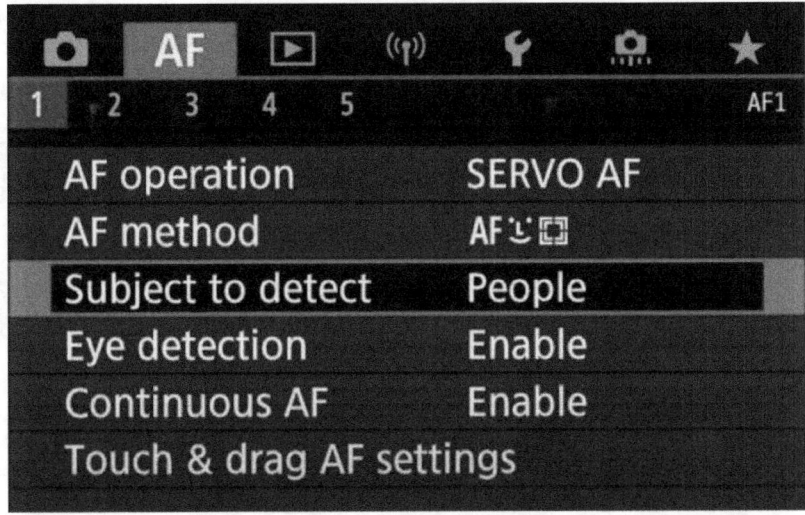

Pick from People, Animals, Vehicles, or None. The camera can focus on certain things, but you can change it by touching the screen.

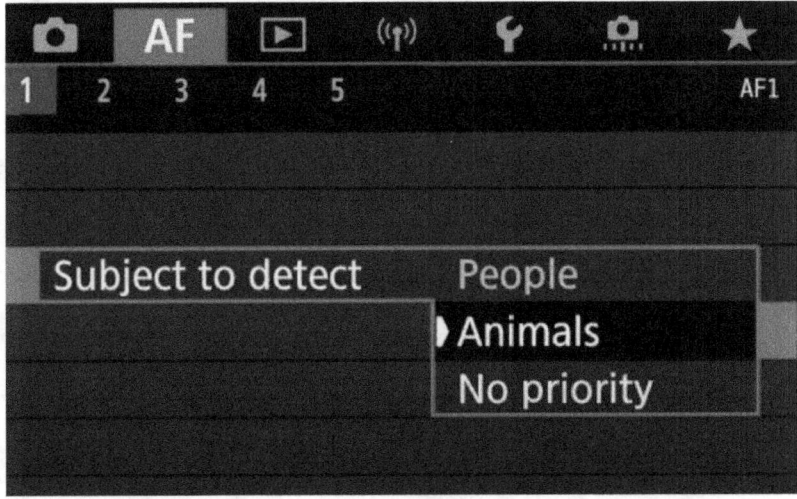

- o **People:** The camera checks for faces or heads first, then looks for the body. It might not find very big or small faces or faces that are partly hidden or too bright/dark.

○ **Animals:** The R10 camera can find dogs, cats, and birds and tries to see their faces or bodies if they're close to the camera. It focuses on animals, not people, making it great for pet photos at events like the Westminster Kennel Club Dog Show.

○ **Vehicles:** This camera setting is excellent for people who like motorsports. It can capture moving cars and bikes, but it might not recognize bicycles or regular cars. Sometimes, dust from races can confuse the camera. You can turn on or off a special feature that helps the camera focus on essential parts of vehicles, like headlights. It can be handy if there are many vehicles close together.

○ **None:** In simple words, this setting makes the R10 camera focus on whatever you're pointing at without showing tracking frames. It won't specifically find faces or eyes.

• **Eye Detection**

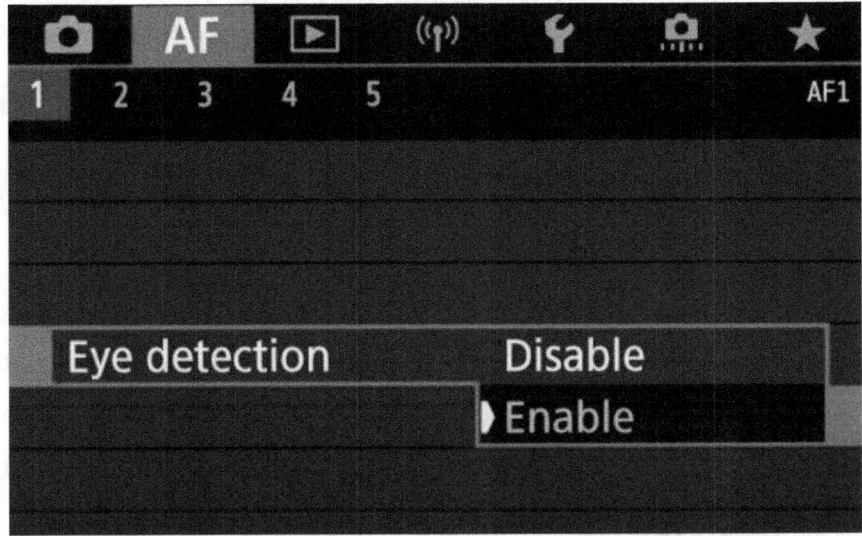

Good eyes can make a photo look great. Canon lets you use eye detection to focus on your eyes, but it takes extra time. You can turn it off if capturing any picture quickly is more important. If you're using Whole Area AF, you can select an eye by tapping the screen.

- **Switching Tracked Subjects**

  This setting decides how fast the camera changes focus when the person you're filming goes out of sight or behind something. If the person turns away or changes their appearance, you might lose focus.

  If needed, the R10 can change topics, and you can decide how long the switch takes. You can choose the delay time.

○ **Initial priority:** The camera tries hard to focus on the first thing it is pointed at, even if other things get in the way.

○ **On subject:** The R10 will try to follow the first subject, but if needed, it will change to follow different subjects after a short wait.

○ **Switch subject:** The camera quickly focuses on different things. It is helpful at a basketball game when the ball moves between players a lot.

Magnified View

You can zoom in and out using 5X or 10X magnification by pressing the Magnify/Reduce button. Press it once or twice to zoom in and a third time to go back to normal view. The zoom focuses on the AF point in certain modes. If you press the shutter button halfway in Spot AF and 1-Point AF, it focuses on the zoomed-in view.

When using different camera settings, focusing works differently. In one setting called Servo mode, the camera shows a regular view to help with focusing. But in zoomed-in views, some focusing options might need to be improved. If the image is shaky, it can be harder to focus. To adjust the zoomed-in view, you can use a button on the camera to move the magnified area around the screen. Pressing the button centers the zoomed-in area in the middle of the screen.

Choosing the AF Area

The Canon EOS R10 has 651 focus positions in its sensor for accurate focusing. In some modes, the camera automatically picks the focus point using face detection. In other modes, you can let the camera choose or choose the focus point yourself from eight options.

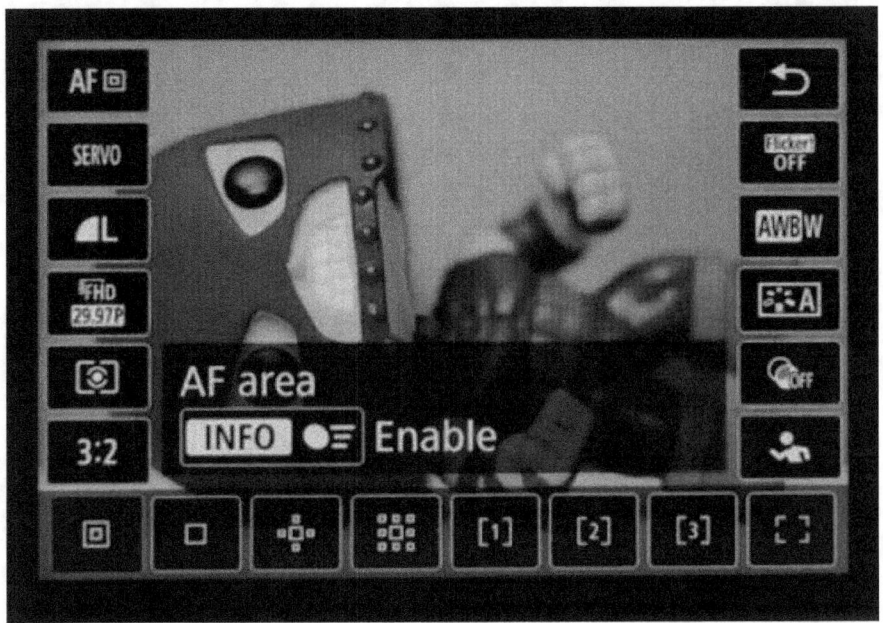

Here are the things :

- **Spot AF**

  In this mode, you can concentrate on a small box on the screen. You can move this box around using the joystick or dial buttons to focus on different areas. Just press the

AF point selection button to start moving the focus point.

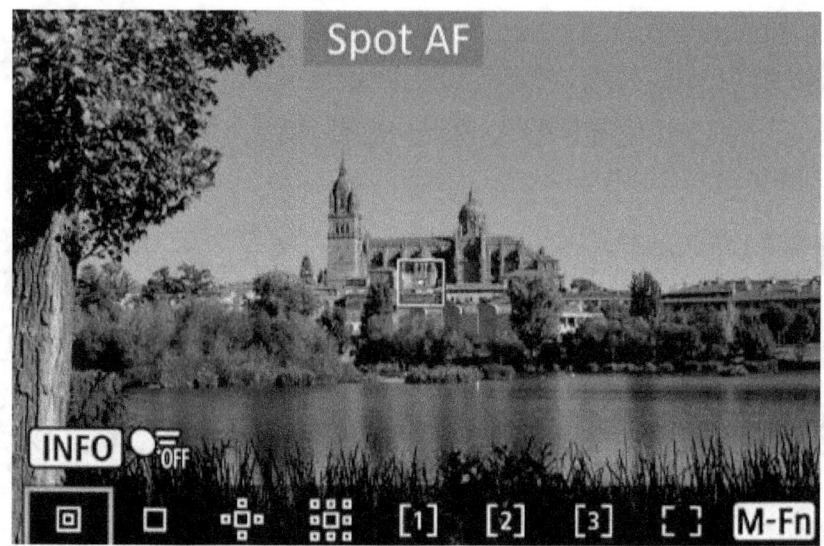

This fancy camera feature lets you focus accurately, but it can be tricky. If you or your subject move, the focus might shift. It's great for detailed subjects or slow-moving scenes. You can use it for everyday photos, too, as long as there's enough detail where you want to focus. But if your subject needs to be clearly defined, other modes can help by considering nearby focus points.

- **1-point AF**

In this mode, you can zoom in on a bigger box on the screen. It's great when you need speed and precision, like in sports, to focus on players who aren't moving much, like an infielder on third base. You can change the focus point too.

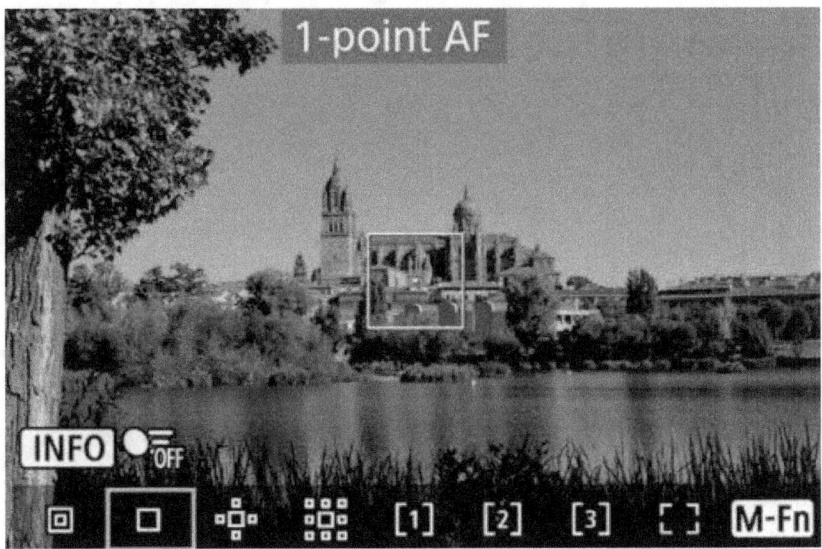

- **Expand AF area**

  In this mode, the point you choose to focus on is used, along with nearby points, to keep track of moving objects within the camera frame. This mode is great for capturing moving subjects because it makes it easier to follow them. If the subject moves away from the chosen focus point, nearby points can continue tracking its movement.

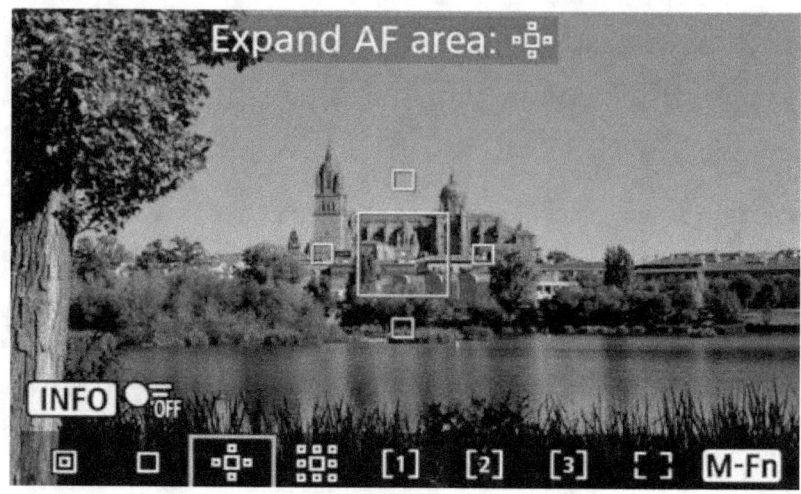

- **Expand AF area: Around**

  This mode is like before, but it includes eight nearby points when you select a point. It works better for simple subjects at the chosen point and for big moving objects. You can move the active area shown in the center of the screen.

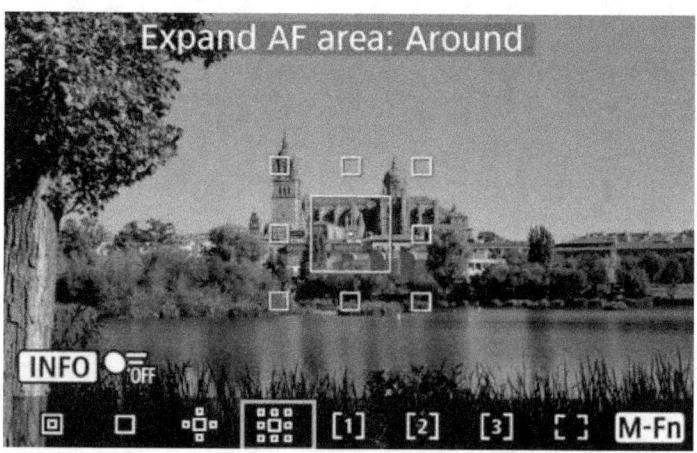

- **Flexible Zone AF 1**

  This method divides the focus area into a square zone. When you move the focus, you move this zone within the frame. It's useful when you have a general idea of where your subject will be. However, it could be more precise than other methods. You can move the zone by pressing a button and using the controls.

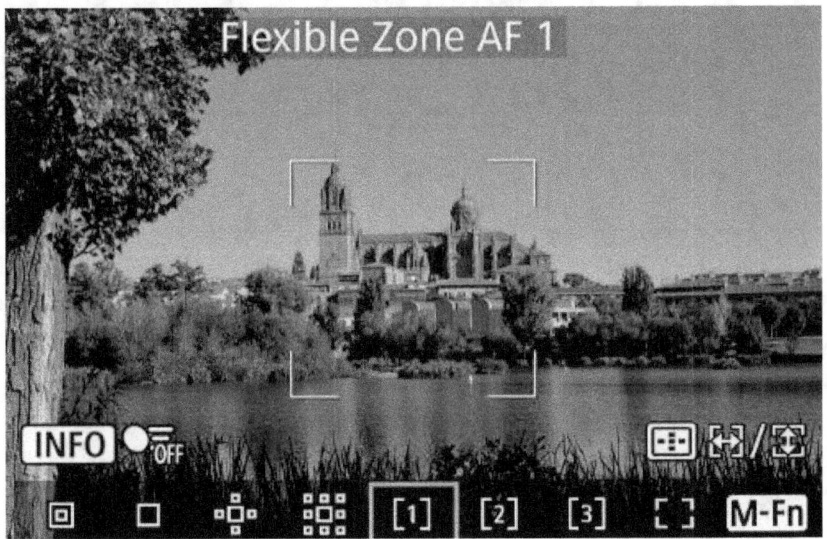

- **Flexible Zone AF 2 (Vertical) / Flexible Zone AF 3 (Horizontal)**

51

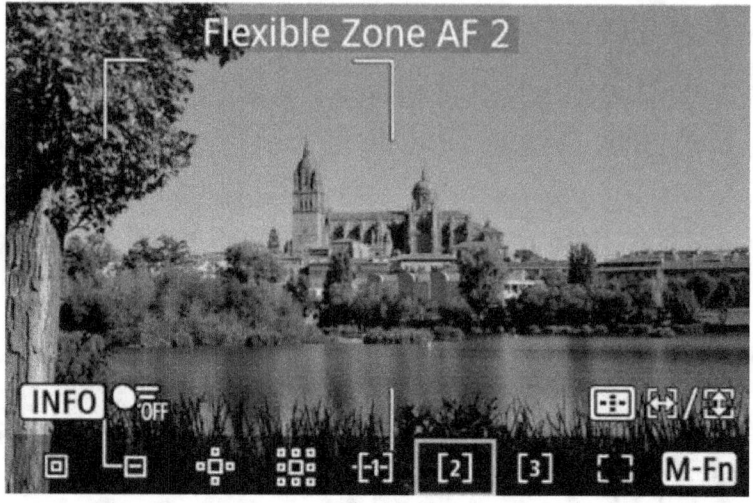

These methods use big rectangular areas that can be tall or wide. You can adjust their size based on what you need. They work well for capturing tall things like basketball or wide scenes like motorsports. The camera automatically chooses the right focus points, even if faces are in the picture.

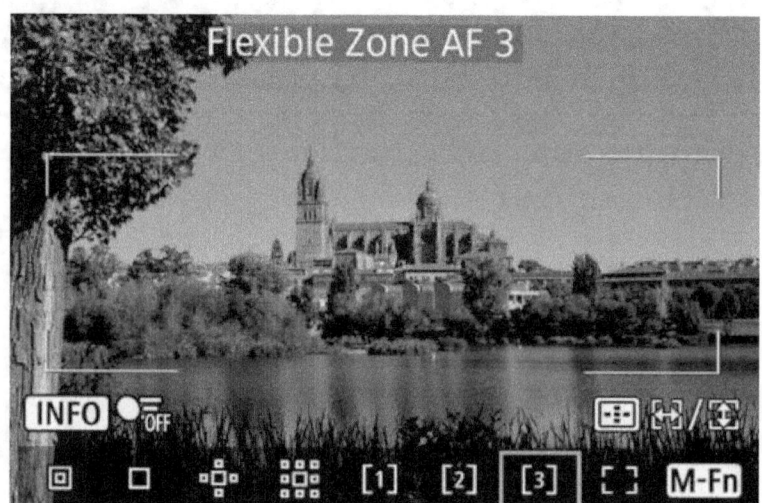

- **Whole area AF**

  In this mode, the camera picks where to focus across the whole picture. It's excellent for fast-moving things where picking a focus spot is hard. I use it for sports. You can also tap the screen to focus on a face or eye when this mode is on with Subject Tracking.

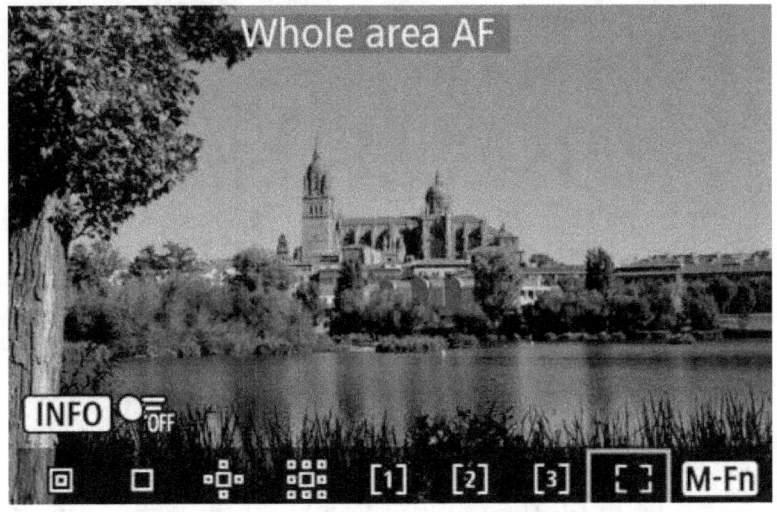

Choosing the AF Method

The R10 camera has different ways to pick where it focuses. Besides the Quick Control menu, here's how you can choose where the camera focuses.

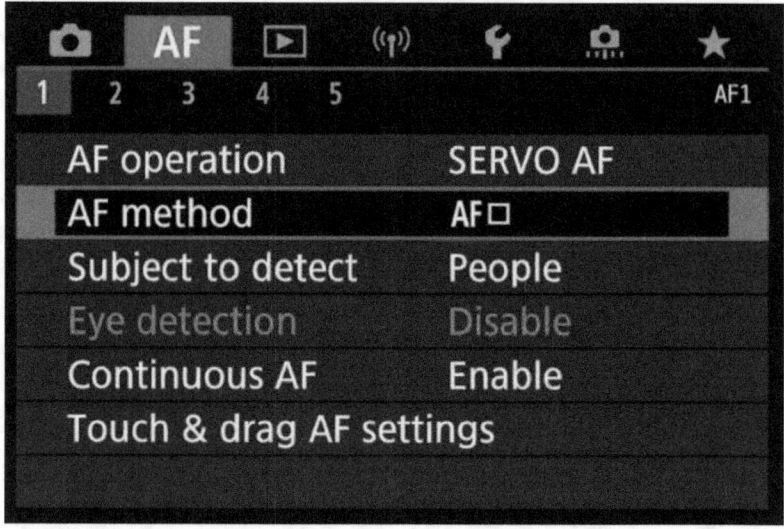

1. Press the button on the back of the camera to choose where the camera focuses. You have to do this every time you want to change the focus area or choose a specific point.

2. After pressing the focus button, quickly press another button on the camera to switch between different focus modes. You can also use dials or directional buttons to do this, whichever you find easier.

3. Choose AF area mode. When you press the M-Fn button, you'll see different options on the screen. The highlighted one is the mode you've chosen—press INFO to turn Subject Tracking on or off. Press SET to confirm your choice.

CHAPTER 3: CHOOSING BASIC PICTURE SETTINGS

Selecting a Shooting Mode

To start, turn on your camera and make sure you have a lens, battery, and memory card. Then, choose the shooting mode, metering mode, and focus mode. Use the Mode Dial on top of the camera to pick the shooting mode you want. The chosen mode will be shown in the viewfinder or LCD screen. If you can't see it, press the INFO button next to the LCD.

The camera has an easy mode called Scene Intelligent Auto (A+ on the screen), where it makes most decisions for you, except when to take the picture. There are other simple options like Special Scene modes (labeled SCN) and Creative Filters (shown as filter icons on the Mode Dial).

Your camera, the EOS R10, has different modes that let you control how it takes pictures. These modes include Flexible-priority, Program, Shutter-priority, Aperture-priority, Manual, and Bulb. You can adjust exposure and settings with these modes. There are also two custom modes (C1 and C2) to save specific settings for quick use. And there's a movie mode located between Creative Filters and C2 slots, represented by a movie camera icon.

If you're starting with digital photography, use the Scene Intelligent Auto or Program mode on your camera. These modes will automatically adjust settings for different shooting situations, making it easier for you to take pictures. Here are your options :

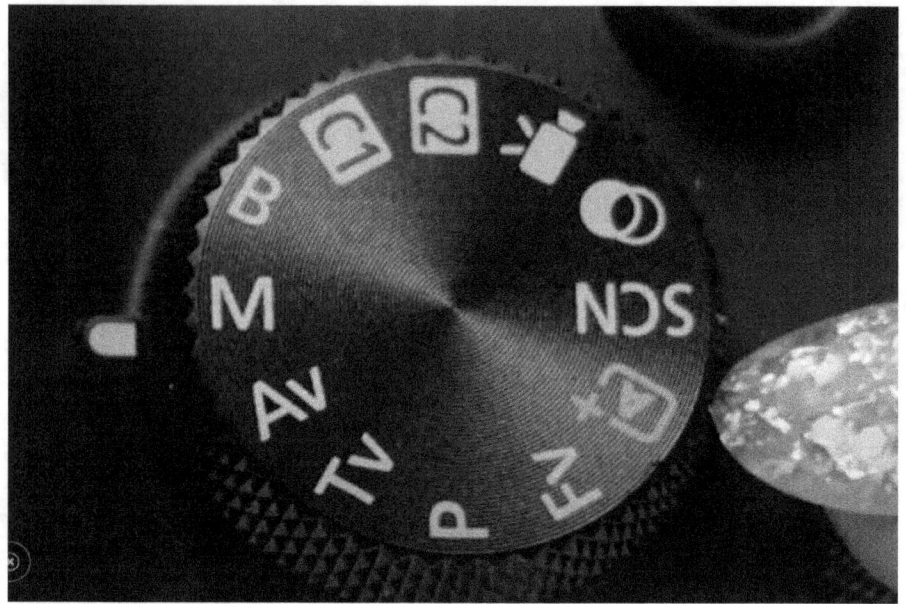

- **A+ (Scene Intelligent Auto):** Scene Intelligent Auto (A+) is a fully automatic mode that makes virtually all the decisions for you (except when to press the shutter). It is a good choice for beginners and for situations where you want the camera to do all the work for you.

- **Special Scene modes:** When you turn the dial to a specific setting, press SET and turn the main dial to pick a shooting mode like Portrait, Landscape, Sports, and more.

- **Creative Filters:** Turn the dial to the right setting, then press SET. Use the Main Dial to pick Grainy B&W,

Soft Focus, Fish-eye, Water Painting, Toy Camera, Miniature, or HDR Art (Standard, Vivid, Bold, and Embossed).

- **Fv (Flexible-priority):** Fv means flexible value. It's a new camera mode that lets you choose one setting (like shutter speed, aperture, or ISO), and the camera figures out the rest. You can set it yourself or let the camera do it. And if your photos are too dark or bright, you can adjust them easily. This choice lets you pick some settings automatically and others by yourself.

- **P (Program):** Program mode (P) is a semi-automatic mode that allows you to control some of the camera's settings, such as the ISO sensitivity and white balance. However, the camera will still automatically set the shutter speed and aperture. Program mode is a good choice for situations where you want more control over the camera's settings, but you don't want to worry about setting everything manually.

- **Tv (Shutter-priority):** This mode (Tv for time value) helps you choose a specific shutter speed to capture fast movements or create blurry effects. The camera picks the right f/stop for you.

- **Av (Aperture-priority):** Pick the lens opening you want to use to control sharpness and focus in your photos. The camera will automatically choose the right shutter speed for you. Av means aperture value.

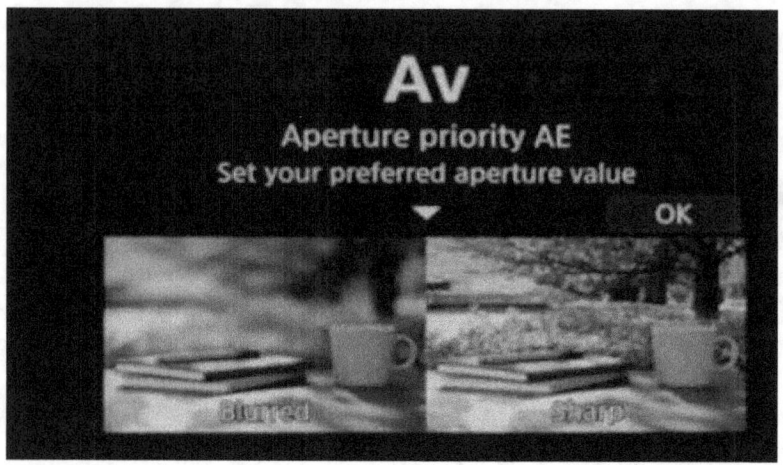

- **M (Manual):** Choose this when you want to control how fast the camera takes a picture and how much light enters the lens. It is helpful for creative purposes or when using specific types of flashes that don't work with automatic settings.

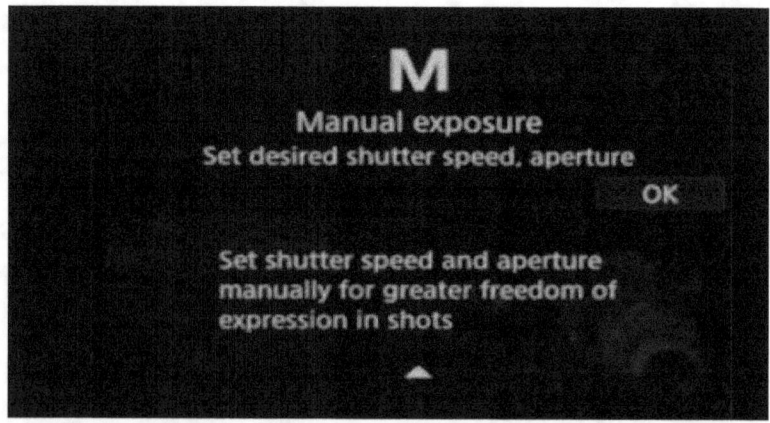

- **B (Bulb):** Select this mode, and the camera will keep taking a picture for as long as you hold the button. It's handy for capturing fireworks, where you want to leave the camera open until the fireworks show up and then close it after a few seconds to capture the light trails. This mode can also take pictures longer than the camera's 30-second limit.

- **Movie:** You can film videos in any mode, but the Movie mode gives you all the specific video settings in the menu.

Selecting a Metering Mode

Choose the metering mode in your camera settings. Ensure your camera is in semi-automatic or manual mode, not Basic Zone modes like Scene Intelligent Auto. The default mode, Evaluative metering, is a good starting point as you learn how your camera works.

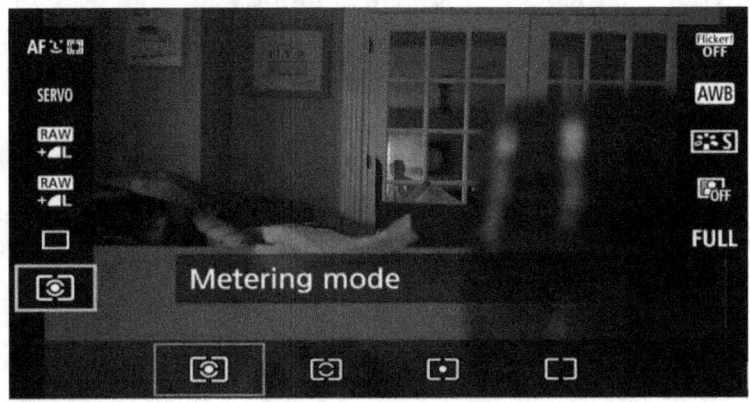

To switch metering modes, go to the Quick Control screen. You can get there differently using these three methods:

Option 1: While looking through the viewfinder:

To change how your camera measures light, go to the Quick Control screen. There are different ways to reach this screen:

1. Turn the camera dial to find the Metering Mode icon at the bottom left.

2. Choose a mode using the main dial.

3. Press SET to confirm your choice.

Option 2: While looking at the LCD screen:

- The screen shows pictures of your subject or information graphics. You can change them by pressing the INFO button.

- If you see the image preview, press the Q/SET button. Then, choose a metering mode on the screen that appears. You can use the touch screen to tap your choice or use the navigational controls for another option.

- If you see the picture on the screen, press the Q/SET button. It will show you a screen with different options, like in Figure 1.10. Look for the Metering Mode icon; it's in the center at the bottom, outlined in orange. Turn the dial to select a mode, then press SET to confirm your choice.

Option 3: When using touch controls:

- Access the Quick Control screen on your device, either the one with pictures or the one with words, as explained in Option 2.

- Just tap the icon on the screen, pick the mode you want, and confirm by tapping the arrow to go back.

CHAPTER 4: TAKING CHARGE OF EXPOSURE

Working with Short Exposures

You can have fun trying quick camera settings to capture cool pictures. You can use a fast flash or high shutter speed. You can change them by pressing the INFO button.

- **Take revealing images:** Using fast shutter speeds in photography helps capture genuine moments by freezing movement. A famous photographer, Philippe Halsman, took jumping photos of famous people, showing their true selves when they were caught off guard. You can try taking quick pictures of people you know while they're doing something else to capture their natural expressions.

- **Create unreal images:** High-speed cameras can capture unreal images. For example, a helicopter's rotating blades can look frozen in one photo taken very quickly, while in another taken a bit slower, the blades look blurry like how we see them usually.

- **Capture unseen perspectives:** Some things are too fast or fleeting to see with our eyes, but we can capture them using special cameras. For example, we can freeze a hummingbird in motion or capture splashes of liquid falling into a bowl. To do this, photographers use bright lights and specific camera settings instead of a regular flash.

- **Vanquish camera shake and gain new angles:** A fast shutter speed can help you take pictures without needing a tripod. You can move around quickly and capture different angles, especially with long lenses. If you have good lighting and use a wide aperture, you can take photos without worrying about a shaky camera. I have a favorite 500mm lens for taking pictures of animals and sports. I usually use a tripod with it. But if I use a breakneck shutter speed and high ISO setting, I can sometimes hold the lens without a tripod and capture fast-moving subjects more easily.

Long Exposures

Taking pictures for a longer time can make ordinary scenes look different. At night, it can capture lights from moving objects like cars or rides. Even in the dark, long exposures can show interesting views using just a bit of light. During the day, long exposures can make moving things disappear in photos, but you might need special filters to do this.

Three Ways to Take Long Exposures

There are three ways to take long-exposure photos: a timer, a bulb mode, or a combination of both. Your camera can do all three. To get clear shots, always use a tripod for stability.

■ Timed exposures. To take a picture in low light, use Manual or Tv modes on your camera. Use the Main Dial to choose how long the camera's shutter stays open, from 1 to 30 seconds. You don't need a stopwatch because the camera calculates your time. If you want to adjust the exposure, you can do it precisely. But you can't take a picture for longer than 30 seconds using this method.

■ Bulb exposures. Bulb exposure means the photographer controls how long the camera's shutter stays open. In the past, they used a bulb attached to a tube. When you press the button, the exposure starts, and it stops when you release the button.

■ Timed bulb exposures. This camera feature lets you take long exposure photos. Look in the camera settings to locate it.

First, set the camera to Bulb mode. Then, go to the Bulb Timer setting in the menu. Enable it and choose how long you want the exposure, up to almost 100 hours. It helps capture things like stars in the sky, especially when you combine multiple shorter exposures into one photo. With this Bulb exposure mode, you press the button, wait a bit, and then take another shot. But it would help if you timed it yourself. If the exposure is short, shaking from opening and closing the shutter might affect the photo. For longer exposures, it's usually okay. You can also use a release cable to avoid shaking the camera.

Working with Long Exposures

Try taking pictures with your camera in the dark using a tripod. See if you like the photos with a special setting turned on or off. Experiment and have fun!

Here are a few things you can do: Here are some things you can try:

- **Make people invisible:** Long exposure photos can make fast-moving things disappear while showing things that stay still. You can do this at night or during the day with special filters. Fast-moving people might vanish, especially if they walk sideways in front of the camera. At night, it's even easier to make things disappear in photos by using long exposure.

- **Create streaks:** If you want cool blurry effects in your photos, use a camera on a stand for a little while. Even in bright sunlight, a special filter lets you do this.

- **Produce light trails:** At night, when cars and other moving lights are around, you can take fantastic pictures of their trails. You don't always need a tripod – holding the camera by hand can make the trails look more attractive with movement. If you capture fireworks or a moving ride at an amusement park, using a tripod and more prolonged exposure can create awesome pictures.

- **Blur waterfalls, etc.:** Waterfalls and flowing water can create a blurry, dreamy effect in photos with slow camera exposure. The water's appearance varies based on how fast it's flowing and how long the camera exposure is. Fast-flowing waterfalls appear rougher, while smooth ones look gentler. Even though blurry waterfalls are common in photos, there are many ways for photographers to be creative and capture unique images.

- **Show total darkness in new ways:** Even on nights, there's still some light from stars or faraway sources. You can see things, and if you use a long camera exposure, you can even take pictures.

Delayed Exposures

Sometimes, you should wait before taking a picture. For example, if you want to be in the photo, you can set the camera to wait for 10 seconds after you press the button. Or if your camera is on a tripod, waiting helps reduce vibrations for a clearer picture, especially with slow shutter speeds. Delayed exposure options will be explained next.

Self-Timer

First, set the timer to 10 or 2 seconds using the Drive mode button. Then, halfway, press the shutter button to focus on your subject. If taking a self-portrait, focus on something at the same distance and use a focus lock.

When you're ready to take the photo, fully press the shutter button. If you choose the 10-second timer, a light blinks for eight seconds, and a sound beeps. In the last two seconds, the beeping speeds up, and the light stays on until the picture is taken. If you turn off the sound in the settings, there won't be any beeping.

If you don't have a tripod and want to take steady close-ups or landscape photos using the self-timer on your camera, find a stable surface like a fence post or rock. Set the self-timer and press the shutter, and the camera might wobble a bit before taking the picture. Remember to turn off the self-timer when you're done.

Time-Lapse and Interval Photography

Have you ever been fascinated by pictures taken at different times to capture an event? Or watched a fast-forward video of a flower blooming or the moon moving? You may have seen videos of long processes like a building being built quickly.

Time-lapse movies	FHD 29.97P ALL-I
Time-lapse	Enable
Interval	00:00:03
No. of shots	0300
Movie rec. size	FHD
Auto exposure	Fixed 1st frame
00:11:57	▶ 00:00:15
	MENU ↵

You likely will only take construction photos if you have an extra camera to set up in the same way for a long time. But you can easily do other types of time-lapse photography.

I took pictures from my office window in Florida using a special camera setting. I left the camera running for hours and captured three images. I also use this setting for taking pictures of sunsets. I aim the camera at the horizon, take three shots with different brightness levels, and capture a new image every 10 seconds.

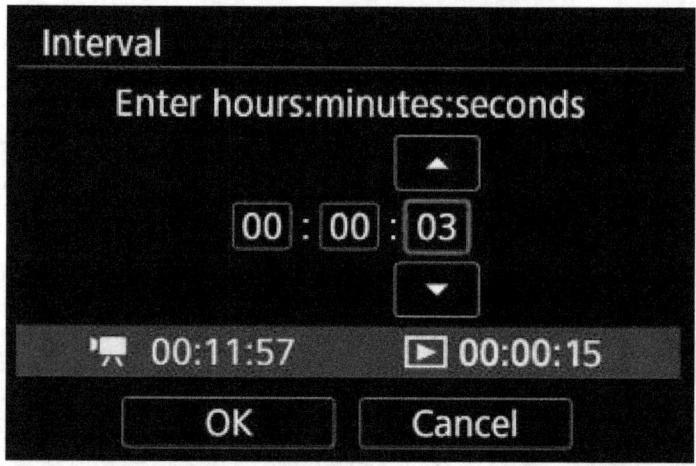

You can easily take pictures at regular intervals and make time-lapse movies using the camera's built-in features. But before I explain how to do it, here are a few essential things to remember.

- **Use AC power:** If you're filming for a long time, use a power adapter for your camera. Keeping the camera on for too long drains the battery quickly. You can use external power sources. Also, during time-lapse shooting, the camera won't turn off automatically.

- **Disabled functions:** When taking time-lapse videos, certain camera features like shooting, menus, and playback are turned off. You can't use digital zoom, sound, or time codes either. The camera won't change focus between shots, and in a specific mode, the aperture stays the same while the exposure adjusts to keep the focus consistent. Also, the video output to HDMI devices is turned off during this process.

  o Make sure your memory card can store all your photos. If it's not big enough, use a lower-quality setting to fit more pictures. For example, a 256GB card can hold 72 minutes of 4K video or 6 hours and 19 minutes of Full HD video.

- **Protect your camera:** If you leave your camera out for a long time, keep it safe from weather, animals, kids, people, and theft.

- **Vary intervals:** Try changing how often you take pictures. Don't do it too much or too little; just enough to capture the changes you want in your videos or pictures. If it takes too long to save a picture, the next one will be skipped.

Star Trails

To capture star trails, use your camera on a still tripod to take long-exposure photos of the night sky. Due to Earth's rotation, stars appear to move, creating light trails in your photos. Using extended shutter speeds, you can capture trails up to 15 minutes long, with trails centered around the North Star in the northern hemisphere and Sigma Octantis in the southern hemisphere.

To capture clear pictures of stars, photographers avoid long exposures because they can cause blurry images and camera overheating. Instead, they take multiple shorter shots and combine them into one picture of the star trails. To prevent stars from looking blurry, there's a simple rule: divide 500 by your lens's focal length. For a 50mm lens, the longest exposure is 10 seconds. Wider lenses, like 16mm, can have exposures of around 30 seconds to capture more stars in one frame.

I took a picture for 90 minutes using my camera set at specific settings. After that, I used Photoshop to edit the picture.

1. Transfer files to a folder. Choose a folder on your computer and move all your files into it.

2. In Photoshop: Click on "Files," then select "Scripts," and finally choose "Load Files into Stack."

3. Browse to folder. Just tap "Browse," then find the folder where your pictures are kept.

4. Click OK. Photoshop will make a file with separate layers for your pictures.

5. First, click on all the layers. Then, go to Layer Blending Options in the Layers menu and pick Lighten.

6. Flatten image. Make your picture flat (so it's a manageable size), and you'll get an excellent star trail photo!

CHAPTER 5: CAPTURING VIDEO

Movie Shooting Menus

Movie Shooting 1 Menu

Shooting Mode

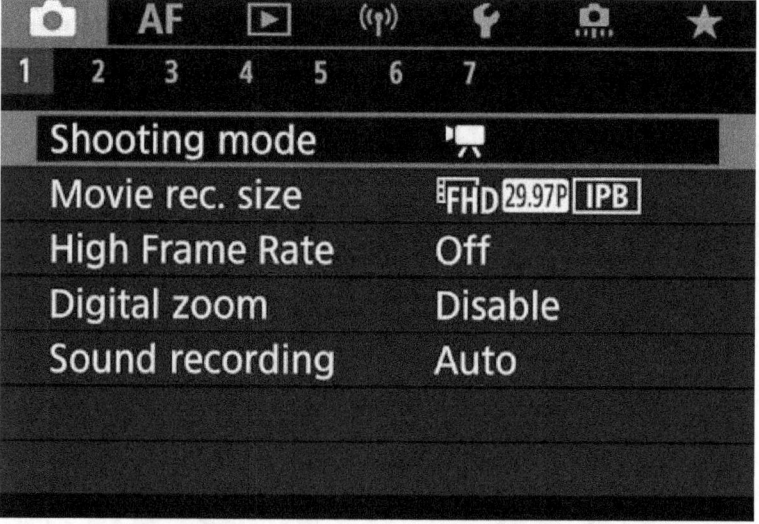

It is the first option in the movie Shooting 1 menu. You can let the R10 set the brightness for you, set it yourself, or choose high-quality video with HDR.

Movie Recording Size

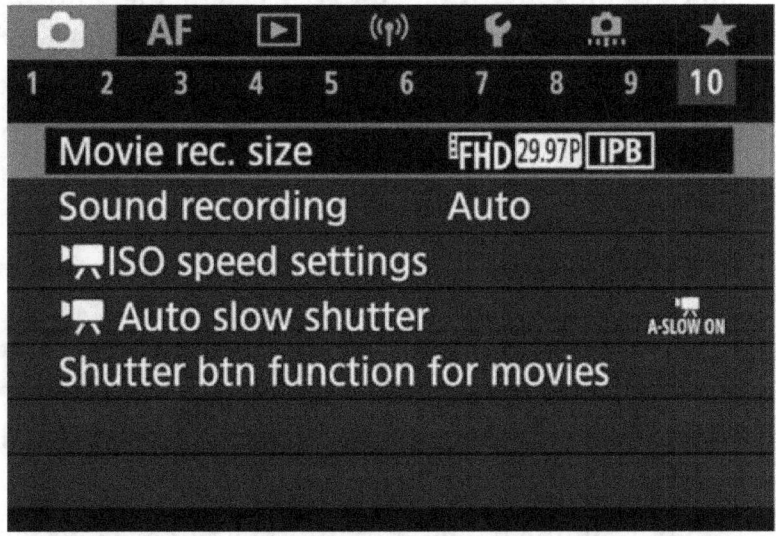

Your camera has different video settings, like super clear 4K video. I'll explain them later, but you can choose from various options.

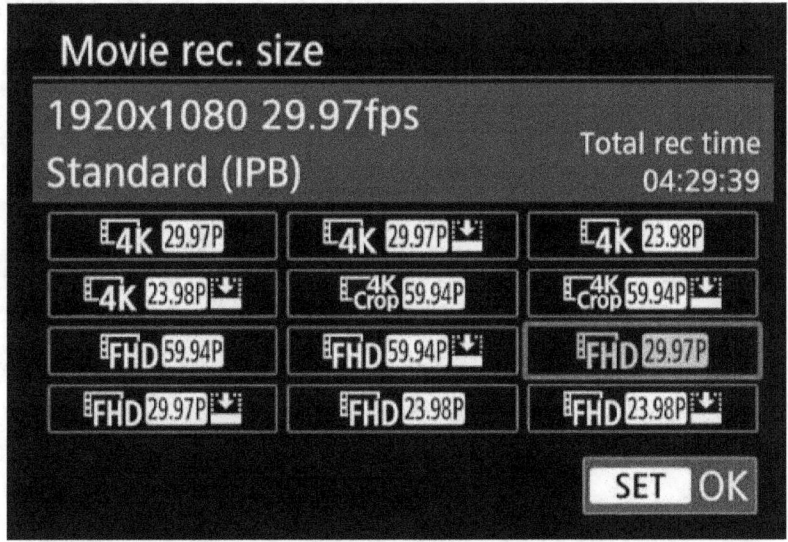

- **Image size:** It means the movie can be clear, like super sharp photos, in 4K or Full HD. The quality and size of the movie can change based on how it's recorded and the camera settings. The R10 camera can record very detailed 4K (3840 × 2160) and Full HD (1920 × 1080) videos. There's also a special mode that makes the 4K video even closer, like zooming in a lot. You can use time-lapse features for both 4K and Full HD videos, too.

- **Frame rate:** It means how many pictures are taken every second in a video. People often say 120, 60, 30, or 24 pictures per second, but the exact numbers can be a bit different, like 119.9 or 59.94. Countries also use different numbers, like 100 or 50 pictures per second in Europe.

Some video settings only work with specific frame rates. For instance, with NTSC, 4K Fine works with 29.97 and 23.98 frames per second, while 4K Crop mode needs a 59.94 frame rate. Regular 4K and FHD support 59.94, 29.97, and 23.98 frames per second. High Frame Rate movies, recorded at 119.9 (NTSC) or 100.0 (PAL), playback at slower speeds.

- **Compression method:** Each picture or video you take is made smaller to save space and make it easier to store. It is done by compressing the files. I'll explain the details later.

Movies are saved in MP4 format, like a digital box for video files. MP4 is a standard used globally and works well. It uses a method called progressive scan. MP4 files end with .MP4.

High Frame Rate

When you turn on High Frame Rate in movies, your video is recorded at a breakneck speed but is played back much slower. For example, one second of the action takes four seconds to playback. If you connect your camera to a screen using an HDMI cable, the video will play back at a slightly faster slow-motion speed, taking two seconds to play back one second of action.

You can record sound, but only up to 1 hour and 30 minutes. Sometimes, the video might flicker in certain types of lighting. The camera settings allow you to use ISO speeds between 100 and 12,800 (or 25,600 if you enable extended settings). There's a feature called High Frame Rate video, which is excellent for capturing slow-motion scenes in your movies or studying movements.

Digital Zoom

When you set the movie size to settings like FHD 29.97, 23.98 (NTSC), or 25 (PAL), you can zoom in digitally up to 10 times. It means the camera enlarges the center of the picture, but it can make the picture noisy and lower its quality.

To use this feature, tap the W/T icon in the lower-right corner of the screen. Then, you can zoom in and out using the up/down buttons.

Sound Recording

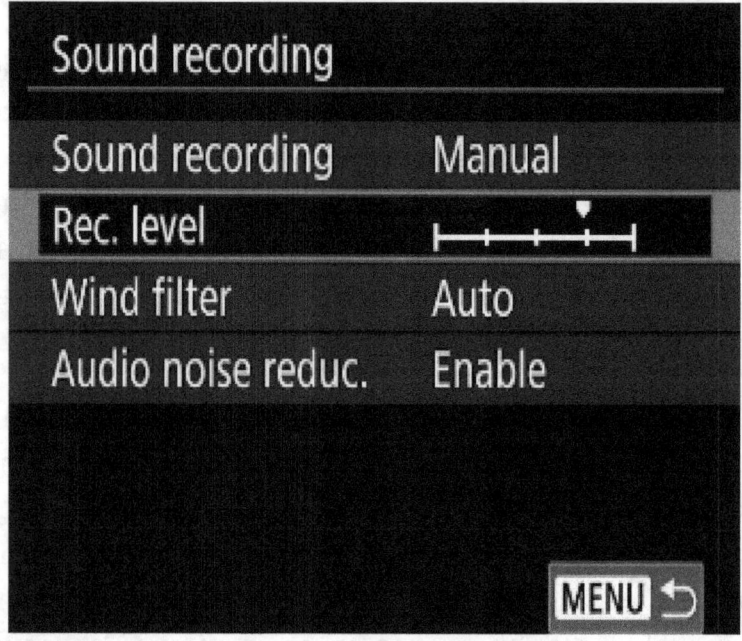

This option allows you to pick Auto, Manual, or Disable. You can also turn on or off the wind filter and audio noise reduction. In Movie Scene Intelligent Auto (A+) mode, you can choose On (Auto level) or Off. You can't adjust the left/right balance.

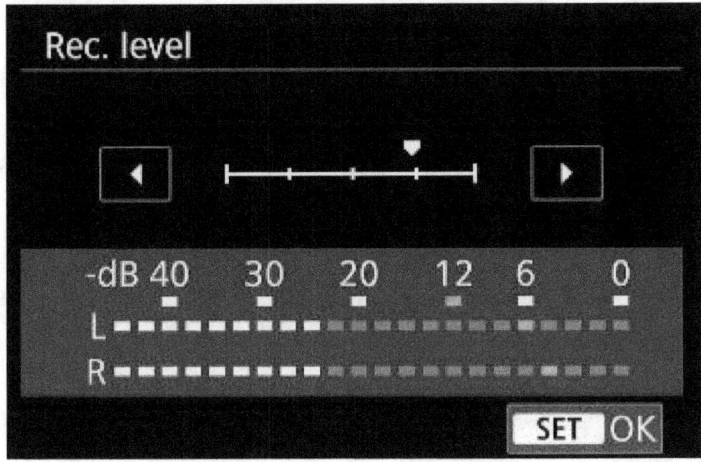

- **Auto:** I've adjusted the sound volume for you

- **Manual:** Pick one of 64 sound levels. Adjust the recording level using the QCD while looking at the meter at the bottom. Aim for an average of -12 dB for loud sounds. Be careful not to reach the 0 point on the scale, or your recording will be distorted.

- **Disable:** Record your video quietly. You can add voices, music, or other sounds later using editing software. If you're connected to another device, like a recorder through HDMI, make sure sound recording is enabled in the camera, or you won't hear any audio.

- **Wind Filter:** Turning off the windy sound filter makes your recordings sound better, especially with no wind. An external microphone with a windshield is an even better way to improve audio quality.

- **Audio Noise Reduction:** This filter reduces the noise made by the camera lens when it's focusing. Some lenses are louder, so use them only when needed, as it can affect sound quality. It also reduces background noise a bit. If you set it to 'High,' it reduces noise more, but it can impact sound quality. For better sound, you can use an external microphone plugged into the camera's side. Built-in microphones might capture camera sounds like the lens moving.

Movie Shooting 2 Menu

Movie ISO Speed Settings

It is the first option in the movie settings menu. It lets you control how bright or dark your videos are. You can choose a specific brightness level or set limits for the camera to adjust automatically.

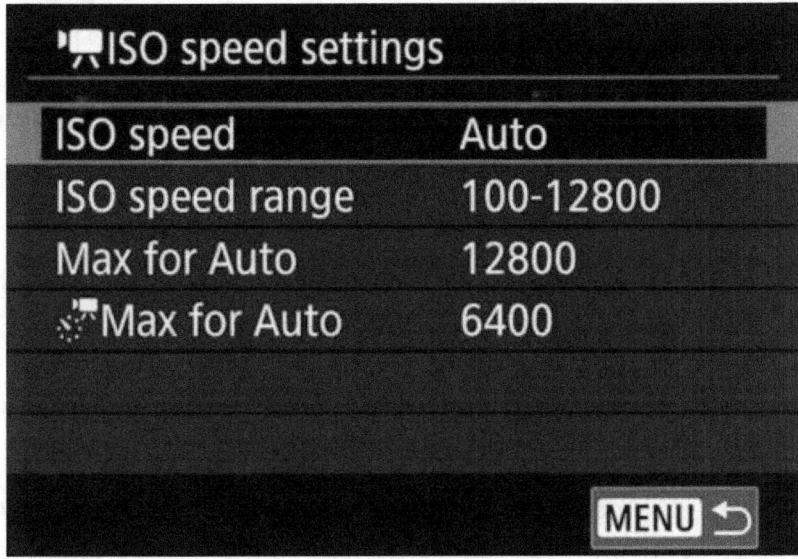

The list has smaller parts called subentries, like this:

- **ISO Speed:** You can change ISO speed only in Manual mode. In other modes, it changes automatically, and you can't adjust it. In Manual mode for movies, you can pick ISO from 100 to 25,600 or let it be automatic.

- In the Manual exposure mode's Auto setting, you can choose the aperture and shutter speed, and the camera adjusts the ISO for the correct exposure. It gives you control over your video's focus and helps you pick the correct shutter speed for your video.

- **ISO Speed Range:** You can choose the lowest and highest ISO settings available.

- ○ **Minimum:** Ensure to adjust how sensitive your camera is to light. You can set it from low sensitivity (ISO 100) to high sensitivity (ISO 12,800) and even higher (ISO 25,600 equivalent).

- ○ **Maximum:** You can set the highest ISO level to 25,600, and the Highlight Tone Priority setting won't change that. I use this feature often to prevent accidental changes. For instance, at concerts, I keep my ISO between 1600 and 6400, depending on the lighting. Outdoors, I might limit it between ISO 100 and 800 in daylight.

- **Max for Auto:** It is like a safety feature for Auto ISO. It sets the maximum limit for ISO operation.

- **Time-lapse Max for Auto:** Choose the highest sensitivity setting for taking high-quality time-lapse videos in different exposure modes. By default, it's set at 12,800, but you can pick any value between 400 and 12,800.

HDR Shooting

This option in the Movie Shooting 2 menu lets you turn on or off HDR movie recording for the next movie you make. It's different from the settings for still photos. You can choose to have HDR on or off or use it with specific settings. Some settings like Auto Slow Shutter, Canon Log, Clarity, and

Creative Filters affect HDR shooting. More details about HDR movies can be found later in this chapter.

Movie Av 1/8-stop Increments

RF-mount lenses have exact aperture control. Canon allows adjusting the f/stops in tiny steps, crucial for consistent movie exposure. This fine adjustment is available in specific modes (Av and M) and can be set to 1/8th-stop increments, providing more control than the usual 1/2- or 1/3-stop adjustments. Note that this feature only works with RF-mount lenses, not EF or EF-S lenses.

Movie Auto Slow Shutter

In easy words, this option in the menu is for movies. It lets the camera use a slower shutter speed in specific modes and frame rates. You can ensure to choose to turn this feature on or off.

- **Disable:** In easy words, this option in the menu is for movies. It lets the camera use a slower shutter speed in specific modes and frame rates. Using this feature or not depends purely on your decision.

- **Enable:** Slower shutter speeds, like 1/30th second, make movies brighter and less noisy. But, if things move, they might look blurry or leave a streak in the video because the camera takes longer to capture the image.

Movie Shooting 5 Menu

Time-lapse Movie

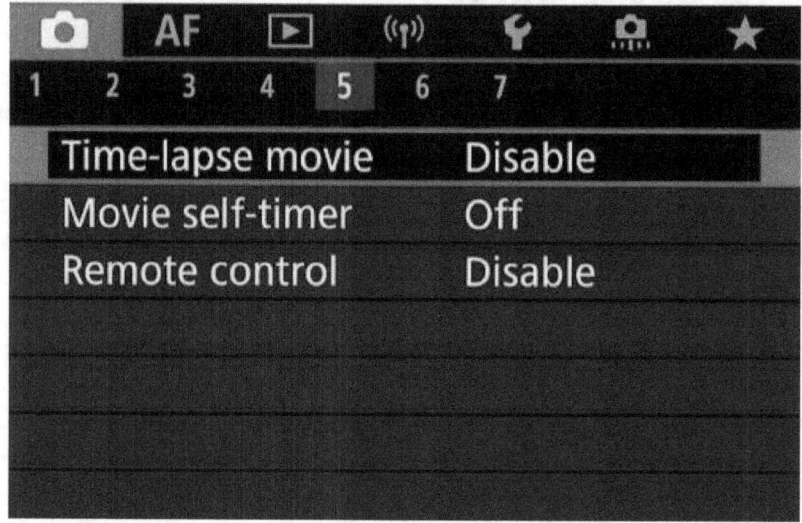

In the Movie Shooting menus of Camera 3 and 4, there are no options for making movie-like videos. So, we'll use the settings in the Movie Shooting 5 menu. Time-lapse photography isn't just for nature lovers capturing flowers blooming. It's widely used in movies and TV shows to show time passing, like the sun moving or seasons changing. Canon allows you to use this cool technique in your videos, too!

Time-lapse movie 📹   FHD 29.97P IPB

Time-lapse	Enable
Interval	00:00:03
No. of shots	0300
Movie rec. size	FHD
Auto exposure	Fixed 1st frame

📹 00:11:57   ▶ 00:00:15

MENU ↩

- **Time-lapse:** Click "Enable" to start setting up, or choose "Disable" to turn off the option.

- **Interval:** You can pick how long to wait between shots, up to almost 100 hours.

- **Number of shots:** Choose how many pictures you want, between 2 and 3,600. The time it takes for all the pictures to be taken will be shown on the screen. If the time is in red, your memory card is too small or incorrectly formatted. Don't worry; most cards are set up correctly in the camera. The recording stops when the card is full, or the file size is too big.

- **Movie Recording Size:** You can pick high-quality video options like 4K or Full HD, with two different frame rates. The video compression method used is the same for all these options.

- **Auto Exposure:** Ensure you select:

  - **Fixed 1st Frame:** Metering takes plvace, and the exposure is set for the first frame and used for all subsequent frames. Use this setting when you want the picture's brightness to stay the same, no matter how the lighting changes.

  - **Each Frame:** Metering means checking the right light for each picture taken in a series. If you're making a time-lapse video of a city skyline from morning to evening, the pictures will be correctly bright for every part of the day.

- **Screen Auto Off:** Scroll down to find the option. You can keep the screen on for 30 minutes without automatic turn-off or turn it off 10 seconds after starting to shoot once you've checked your framing and exposure.

- **Beeps per Image Taken:** Turn on or off the sound when a picture is taken in time-lapse mode.

Movie Self-timer

This feature lets you delay video recording by either 10 or 2 seconds. It gives you time to prepare yourself in front of the camera. Choose 10 seconds if you need extra time, like combing your hair, and 2 seconds if you're ready. It's helpful if you need a remote control for the camera. Vloggers could use it for spontaneous videos, but skilled users might edit out any rushed parts later.

Remote Control

To use a remote control for your camera, you have to turn on your camera first. The R10 works with the Wireless Remote Control BR-E1. Check your remote's manual to understand what each device can do.

Movie Shooting 6 Menu

IS (Image Stabilizer Mode)

It is the first option in the movie Shooting 6 menu. Even if your camera already has stabilization in specific lenses, it can also use a feature called Movie Digital IS for extra stability when recording videos.

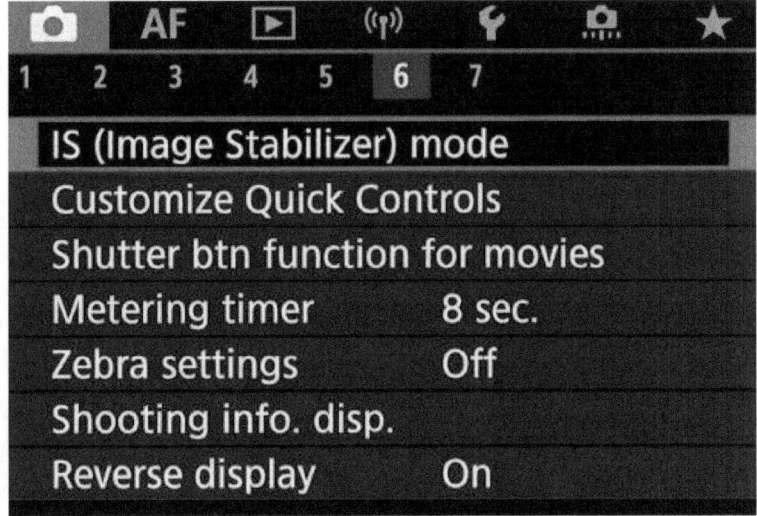

Movie digital image stabilization uses extra image information around the video frame. When the camera detects movement, it shifts the whole frame slightly to keep the main subjects steady. This process trims the edges of the frame, making the video slightly zoomed in.

Movie Digital IS helps reduce camera shake when shooting videos. It can work with any lens, stabilizing lenses without built-in stabilization. If your lens already has stabilization, Movie IS will work together with it and the camera's stabilization for even better results. Just turn on your lens's stabilization for it to work properly. Canon has a list of compatible lenses for this combined stabilization, but it only works with at most 800mm or specific types like tilt/shift, fish-eye, or third-party lenses.

Here are your choices:

- **IS Mode (On, Off):** If your camera lens doesn't have stabilization, a setting lets you decide if the camera's built-in stabilization is on or off. If you're using a tripod, it's a good idea to turn it off so the camera doesn't make unnecessary adjustments. But if you're holding the camera, it's best to keep it on for steady shots.

- **Movie Digital IS (Off, On, Enhanced):** This choice shows up whether your lens has IS or not. It's the only option if your lens has IS.

    - **On:** This setting fixes shaky camera shots, but it trims the picture's edges, making it a bit bigger. It's best for wide-angle lenses.

- ○ **Enhanced:** If the camera shakes a lot, it's fixed this way, but the picture might look blurry and noisy. Do this only if nothing else is effective.

Shutter Button Function for Movies

This setting lets you decide what the camera's shutter button does while recording a video. It can be different from your usual button settings, and you can customize what happens when you press the button halfway or down.

Half-press

You can choose:

1. **Metering plus Movie Servo AF:** Use this when you want the camera to keep focusing on a moving subject. Press the shutter button to make the camera track and focus on the subject continuously.

2. **Metering plus One-Shot AF:** If you don't want the camera to refocus, use this setting constantly. It's useful for still shots where only the camera moves. Press the shutter button once to focus on your subject, and it stays focused.

3. **Metering Only:** Select this when you only want to measure the light using the shutter button. It won't focus on the camera; it just measures the light.

Fully-press

You can choose:

- **Start/Stop Movie Recording:** It means you can press the camera button down to start or stop recording a video. It's helpful because you can use the same button for taking pictures and recording videos. Assigning video recording to this button is a good choice because you can't take pictures while recording videos, but you can still capture single frames from your videos if you want a still photo.

- **No function:** When it's set like this, pressing all the way doesn't do anything.

Zebra Settings

This tool helps you avoid overly bright parts in your photos. It's like the blinking alerts on digital cameras that show blown-out areas after you take a picture. Zebra patterns are better because they warn you before taking the photo and let you decide how it is too bright. Professionals use it in video shooting, measured in IRE, a signal-level unit.

If you want to use Zebra pattern warnings, go to a menu and pick a pattern and a brightness level, usually between 5 and 100. Then, check your screen, and if the highlights are too bright, change your camera settings.

How bright is too bright? If your camera shows a pattern when the brightness is set to 100 IRE, your image is too bright, and details are lost. For natural skin tones, aim for 70 to 90 IRE.

Caucasian skin is around 80 IRE, darker tones are around 70, and very fair skin can reach 90 IRE. Adjust the camera settings to avoid overexposing and losing details in your photos.

- **Zebra:** Select On if you want to see Zebra patterns while recording a movie and Off if you don't

- **Zebra Pattern:** There are two types of Zebra patterns: lines slanting to the right and lines slanting to the left. They show up in areas that are brighter than what you set. You can choose to see both patterns overlapping, which helps you spot areas that are too bright for both levels.

- **Zebra 1 Level:** You can adjust the Zebra 1 display between 5% and 95%, with a 5% leeway in either direction.

- **Zebra 2 Level:** You can set the Zebra 2 level between 50% and 100%.

Shooting Information Display

The Shooting Information Display and Viewfinder Display Format in the Movie Shooting menu work the same as in Still Photography. Any changes you make in either mode apply to both modes. The only difference is in the Shooting Information Display – the movie version doesn't have the Viewfinder Vertical Display option, even if it's enabled in still mode.

Reverse Display

If the camera's default settings for color don't look right, you can change it. You can either pick from a few options like sunny or cloudy, or you can create your custom setting to get the colors you want.

Movie Shooting 7 Menu

Standby: Low Resolution

It is like the second option in the movie Shooting 7 menu. It's like a mode that helps prevent the camera from getting too hot or using too much power. In this mode, the camera's sensor and memory card are always on while watching or recording videos. It also keeps autofocus and other features active.

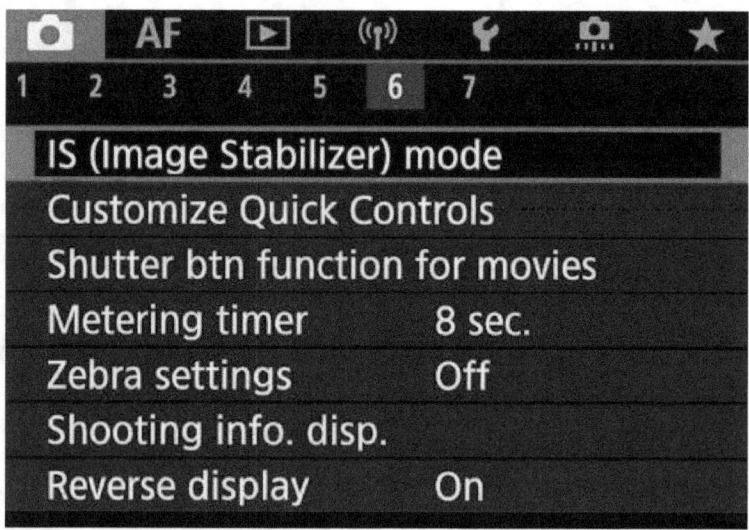

When you record high-quality videos, the camera can get hot because it works fast. This setting helps keep the camera from getting too hot when it's not in use by showing a lower-quality preview image. It saves power, lets you use the camera longer, and doesn't affect your final recorded video much. You can't use this option with Digital Zoom on. If you're not worried about overheating, change it from On to Off.

HDMI Display

When you connect your camera to another device, you can decide if the video shows on both the camera and the other device or just on the other device.

- **Camera+External:** In this mode, the movie you're shooting appears on the camera and another device connected with an HDMI cable. However, you can't record it on the camera's memory card. The HDMI device shows only the video without any extra information, and it's used for showing menus and playback. On the camera, you can see the video being captured and additional info by pressing the INFO button, but menus and playback won't show up. This mode is useful to monitor your recording on both the camera and a distant HDMI-connected device.

- **External Only:** It means the camera only displays videos, info, menus, and images on an external device, not on the camera screen itself.

Time Code

Professional video editors use special codes in videos to help them edit accurately. These codes show the exact time and frame of each moment in the video. They even account for tiny differences in frame rates, making sure everything matches up correctly. It's like a detailed roadmap for editing videos.

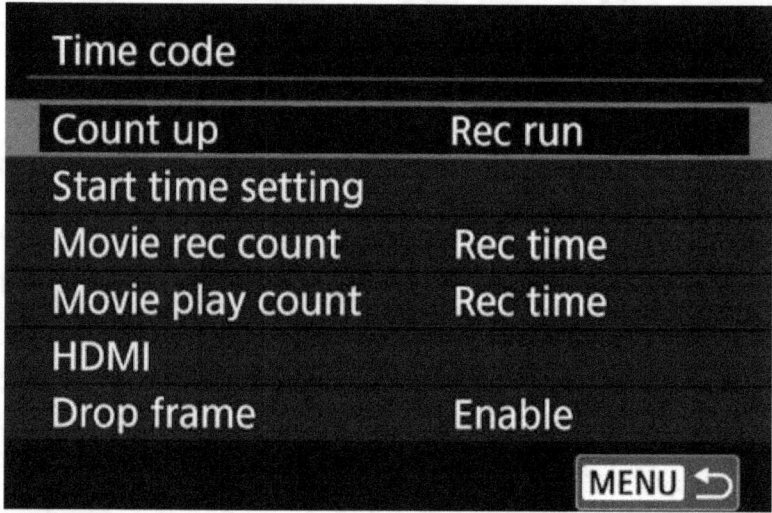

At the beginning of this book, I mentioned that I won't be going into very technical details of movie shooting, like time codes and raw HDMI streaming. If you already know time codes, this book isn't for you. But I will discuss the options in the Time Code submenu, as shown in Figure 16.16.

- **Count Up:** There are two ways to track time when recording videos. One way counts time only when you're recording, and the other keeps track of time all the time, even between recordings. The second method is proper when multiple cameras are recording the same event, and you want to sync their footage later. It helps you edit the videos to match up perfectly, even if the cameras start recording at different times. When you use the second method, the time information is always saved with the video, except for certain types of clips.

It means you can change the time the camera starts recording. Usually, it starts at 00 hours, 00 minutes, 00 seconds, and 00 frames. But you can set it to any time or reset it to the beginning.

- **Movie Rec. Count:** You can show how long the current video clip is on the screen or the Time Code while recording the video.

- **Movie Play Count:** You can pick either elapsed time or Time Code while playing.

- **HDMI:** Sure, if you turn on "Enable," the time code will be added to the video you see on your HDMI screen. If you turn it off ("Disable"), the time code won't be added. When it's enabled, the camera's start and stop actions match with the external recording device. When disabled, the external device controls when the camera starts and stops recording.

- **Drop Frame:** When you pick 30 fps, you get around 29.97 frames per second. For 60 fps, it's about 59.95 frames per second. High Frame Rate (HFR) gives you 119.9 fps. It can mess up the time recording. If you enable a setting, the camera will skip some time codes to fix this. If you turn it off, you might notice a few seconds difference every hour.

Compression, Resolution, and Frame Rates

Compression

The camera uses a standard method called H.264/MPEG-4 to store files. There are two compression options: ALL-I and IPB (Standard or Light), depending on your chosen Movie Size.

ALL-I (All Intraframe)

When you take time-lapse videos, there's a mode that makes it easier to edit them later. In this mode, the camera squeezes each frame you shoot to save space on your memory card. It's like turning each frame into a smaller picture. Even though it doesn't save space as efficiently as other methods, the files are more straightforward to work with when you edit them.

IPB (Standard)

This new method, approved by Canon, compresses videos by saving specific key frames completely, while other frames are created by guessing what happens between those keyframes. The keyframes are called I-frames and are complete images. P-frames only record changes from the previous frame, like a moving person against a still background. B-frames are created by comparing differences from both the previous and next frames. This technique makes videos slightly lower in quality and uses more processing power, but the files are smaller.

To make videos work with your editing software, you must change the format if it's encoded using IPB. This method might make videos look less clear, especially in fast-moving scenes. I use it only when I need to shoot for a long time.

IPB (Light)

It's saved in a way that makes files smaller and faster to share. It is good if you don't need super high quality.

On smaller memory cards (32GB or less), movies can only be 4GB in size due to a specific file system. When a video hits this limit, the camera splits it into smaller parts. To watch or edit the full video, you must view these parts separately or combine them in a movie editor.

SDXC cards, which hold much data, use a special format called exFAT. It allows files to be huge, more than 4GB. But your computer might have limits on how big these files can be.

Resolution

Resolution choices refer to the sharpness of a video. There are two common ones:

1. 4K (3840 × 2160): This is clear and the future standard, but not all devices can show it perfectly yet. Even if you

plan to make regular HD videos, starting with 4K can give better quality when you convert it later.

2. 1920 × 1080 (1080p): Also known as "full HD," it's the best quality most TVs and monitors can show. Use this for your important videos, especially if you edit them for DVDs.

Frame Rate

In digital cameras, when shooting videos, there are two main options: 60 frames per second (fps) and 30 fps, used in places like North America, Japan, and Korea, where the NTSC TV standard is followed. The other option is 50 fps and 25 fps, used in Europe, Russia, China, Africa, and Australia, following the PAL standard. The choice depends on where you are, and there's no need to worry about interlaced scans anymore.

There are different speeds at which videos can be recorded. One speed is 24 frames per second (fps), which is typical for movies. However, in reality, it's around 23.976 frames per second. Another speed is 30 fps, used for standard video in places like the US and Japan, but it's actually around 29.97 frames per second. Some cameras can even record at very high speeds, like 120 fps. The choice between these speeds depends on whether you're making a movie or a regular video. Editing software can convert between these speeds.

Shooting your movie at 24 frames per second (fps) makes it look like a film with great detail. But if your video has moving things or if you move the camera, it can look shaky. Using 30 or 60 fps gives a smoother, less shaky home video look on screens. Try both rates and pick the one that works well with your editing software.

Different cameras work in different ways. Some capture images one line at a time, which can cause issues if things are moving. It is called a rolling shutter. Professional cameras capture the whole picture at once, avoiding this problem. If your camera doesn't have this feature, be careful when taking pictures of moving things.

CONCLUSION

The Canon EOS R10 User Guide is a comprehensive resource for anyone who wants to learn how to use the Canon EOS R10 mirrorless camera. It covers everything from basic setup to advanced features, and it is written in a clear and concise style that is easy to understand.

The book begins with a brief introduction to the camera, including its key features and benefits. It then goes on to explain how to set up the camera and prepare it for shooting. This includes topics such as inserting a memory card, charging the battery, and connecting a lens.

Once the camera is set up, the book provides detailed instructions on how to take photos and videos. It covers all of the major shooting modes, including Program Auto, Manual, and Aperture Priority. It also explains how to use the camera's various features, such as its autofocus system, exposure compensation, and white balance.

In addition to basic photography and videography, the book also covers more advanced topics such as using custom functions, shooting in RAW format, and connecting the camera to a computer. It also includes a troubleshooting section that can help users resolve common problems.

Basically, the Canon EOS R10 User Guide is an excellent resource for anyone who wants to learn how to use the Canon EOS R10 mirrorless camera. It is well-written, informative, and easy to use.

www.ingramcontent.com/pod-product-compliance
Lightning Source LLC
Chambersburg PA
CBHW062349290526
45794CB00005B/2148